SECRETARIAL PRACTICE MADE SIMPLE

SECRETARIAL PRACTICE MADE SIMPLE

Betty Hutchinson

A MADE SIMPLE BOOK

Doubleday

NEW YORK LONDON TORONTO SYDNEY AUCKLAND

A Made Simple Book
Published by Doubleday, a division of
Bantam Doubleday Dell Publishing Group, Inc.,
666 Fifth Avenue, New York, New York 10103

Made Simple and **Doubleday** are trademarks of Doubleday,
a division of Bantam Doubleday Dell Publishing Group, Inc.

Library of Congress Cataloging in Publication Data

Hutchinson, Betty.
  Secretarial practice made simple.

  Includes index.
  1. Office practice. I. Title.
HF5547.5.H88 1985   651.3′741   84-18787
ISBN 0-385-19430-7

4 6 8 9 7 5 3

BG

CONTENTS

PART III: INSIDE THE COMPANY / 73

PART IV: LETTER AND MEMO SKILLS   / 131

INTRODUCTION

The Bureau of Labor Statistics recently conducted an extensive study of American labor-force projections for the 1980–90 decade. Of all the occupations in American business, industry, and government, the one in which the largest number of new job openings will occur is that of secretary. As of 1980 there were nearly 2,500,000 people working as secretaries in the United States; an additional 750,000 secretaries will be needed by 1990. An equal number will leave the work force during the decade due to retirement, illness, or other reasons. This means that well over a million people will find employment as secretaries between now and the end of the decade. The same growth trend will carry on into the 1990–2000 period.

These figures do not include the 2,500,000 people who perform general office work. Many of these people will have the opportunity to upgrade their skills and their level of employment to secretary.

This book was written using the following points to guide what was covered and how it was expressed:

1. A secretary is a professional. As a professional, you want to perform the many and varied responsibilities of secretarial work with competence, confidence, and style.

2. Some secretaries will move to different responsibilities in a company—often becoming executives themselves; others will look on their secretarial job as "something to do" while waiting for something else to come up. The great majority of secretaries know the worth of what they do and want to increase the level of their professionalism. Regardless of which kind of secretary you are—one with hopes for something greater that might come from your job, one in passing, or one for whom it is a chosen career—*Secretarial Practice Made Simple* will enable you to raise the level of secretarial practice in your own setting. This will be beneficial both for your company and your boss, and it will certainly make your life at the office easier and more satisfying and rewarding.

3. Both females and males are splendid secretaries. I do not presume that you are a woman. Since you can be either a man or a woman, my discussion on services you can perform to smooth the work and life of your boss is not related to sexist roles or hang-ups.

4. Both females and males are splendid executives. I do not presume that your boss is a man. In one chapter I refer to the boss as "her," in the next I call the boss "him." I think that's smoother than the "him or her" or "she/he" styles some writers use. Also, I wish there were a word in general English use that had fewer emotional overtones than "boss," but all the alternatives I can think of are even less satisfactory or too restricted.

5. The office environment is in a period of great change, due to the introduction of electronic communications of all sorts, ranging from electronic typewriters and word processors to personal computers and electronic mail. Not all offices, nor all executives, have embraced this technology. Certainly there is no standard level of application. But the technology is steadily—and increasingly—affecting a secretary's work. I discuss this new environment from time to time and where appropriate. If you work in such an office, these comments will make sense to you; if your office does not as yet use these means of communication, these comments will alert you to what is probably soon coming your way. The silicon chip is changing the office scene every bit as much as the Remington typewriter did a century ago.

6. Many secretarial handbooks contain extensive lists of words, grammatical rules, proper forms of address, and the like. I provide you with a selected list of such books for ready reference. In this book, however, I concentrate on how to undertake the many elements that make up a secretarial job description rather than focus on language usage.

7. The list of tasks a secretary must perform is extensive. *Secretarial Practice Made Simple* covers the primary tasks you undertake each day. One mark of a skilled professional secretary is the ability to move from one task to another instantly and with ease. You may wish to have every minute of your day pre-planned and fully under your control. But it just doesn't work that way. As you are well into a pressing task, you may be interrupted by the telephone, by visitors, by unexpected job assignments from your boss—sometimes of an urgent character because something came up that no one expected when the day began. You must handle these secretarial roles with flexibility and grace, while continuing to carry through on your known priorities and routines.

8. To grow in professional competence, you will need to develop some skills you do not at present have or have only in part. Skills and knowledge you should acquire or strengthen include typing, word processing, possibly shorthand or speed writing, language usage, and your knowledge of general office procedures. I suggest ways in which you can secure additional training (with a word of caution about the value of such training compared with on-the-job development and guided professional reading). The exact areas you need to develop depend entirely on you and your background, the nature of the work you do, and your ambitions. I give an overall introduction to career enrichment, but you need to tailor-make it for yourself.

The secretary I had in mind as I wrote this book was a composite of several people I have worked with, hired and trained, or sought from other departments to work with me. Some of these people are college graduates; some entered the work force right out of high school. Some of them had always wanted to be excellent secretaries; that role in the company was the career goal they had set for themselves. Others wanted quite a different ultimate career, but worked as secretaries to support themselves and to gain experience in an office environment or in a particular company or industry. Many of these people moved in the career direction of their choice because they were spotted by someone in the company who recognized they were responsible workers. Others were transferred to the areas they wanted to be in because I valued them and the excellent work they had done for me and recommended their promotion. Whichever you are—one who wants a secretarial career or one who wants to be a good secretary as part of preparing for the next step—you will be able to serve your career, your boss, and the company better by putting into practice the suggestions you find in this book.

Most importantly, you spend one-third of each working day in your office. That's too much of your time and energy to take casually. You should be basically happy with what you do and with the people with whom you work. *Secretarial Practice Made Simple* is intended to enable you to feel good about the work you do—to enable you to do it well and with personal satisfaction. You will contribute to a good working relationship with your boss and your colleagues when you do your work professionally and enjoy that sense of accomplishment; and that good working relationship in turn will make it easier to do your job professionally.

In the course of my own working life, I have been an office worker, a secretary, an executive secretary, an assistant to a chief executive officer of a large international firm, a supervisor of secretarial services in a large corporation, an executive with my own secretary, and have founded my own company and serve as its president. It is my strong conviction that business and industry cannot exist without secretarial expertise performed with sensitivity and good judgment. *Secretarial Practice Made Simple* contains what I tried to be, what I trained many to become, and what I want to have in colleagues who work with me. It really is simple, yet it is also the work of a lifetime to keep growing and meeting the challenges of new opportunities.

SECRETARIAL
PRACTICE
MADE
SIMPLE

PART I
THE RIGHT BEGINNING

Whether you are an experienced secretary starting work with a new company or a new boss, or a beginning secretary starting your first assignment, there are several essential principles you should keep foremost in mind during the first few weeks. These basic principles concern what you do, how you do it, and how you relate to other people in the company.

CHAPTER 1
FIRST DAYS

Perhaps the very question to address is "What is a secretary?" The dictionary gives some leads, but touches only the main points. It speaks of someone who handles correspondence, maintains records and files, and ensures that numerous details are taken care of in the efficient running of an office. In some instances, the secretary—often called a "general secretary"—is the officer who administers an organization, such as the United Nations, or a governmental department, such as the Secretary of State. In many countries, the senior civil service officers are called Permanent Secretaries, as contrasted with "Ministers" who change with the varying political winds.

This more administrative note in the secretarial role suggests strongly that your job can be a blend of caring for the paperwork flow of your boss and, at the same time, doing whatever is helpful in enabling him better to administer his work. The more you develop these administrative skills, the more he will probably delegate routine administrative tasks to you. Unlike an assistant executive, you do not have your own line of command in an organizational chart; rather, you serve as an extension of your boss, as an enabler whose work allows him to concentrate on the major matters while you handle routines and details for him.

> **TIP**
>
> The most important assignment regarding your job description is to make sure that both you and your boss have the same concept of what your job should be.

YOUR JOB DESCRIPTION

The most important assignment regarding your job description is to make sure that both you and your boss have the same concept of what your job should be. If he thinks of you only as a monitor of the paper chase, he will resist and probably resent any efforts on your part to help relieve him of administrative routines. On the other hand, if he wants you to assume increasing responsibility for administrative routines, and you consider your job only as taking care of his correspondence and files, he will feel you are falling down on the job and not rising to meet his expectations. Before long he will start looking for someone else who can "really help" him, and you will wonder what went wrong because you thought you were doing the job well.

So, in your initial interview or during your first day or so on the job, ask to talk with him about what you both want the job to be. He may never have had a secretary before, or he may never have used one in other than a restricted paper-centered way. The idea that you can help relieve him of many time-consuming routine tasks may be a new one to him. Or he may want this relief to take place, but wants to transfer these matters to you slowly to see how well you can assume them before he gives you more. If you can talk about your expectations and his expectations, and about any time periods during which you learn certain parts of the job before being given more, you will both find yourselves working together in defining the nature of the job. This is so much better than your both having to guess at what it is you each expect of the other—and never really guessing entirely right.

This kind of discussion early in your relationship also will help establish a freedom in being able to talk openly and frankly about work matters. In many ways, you will be his eyes and ears in the company, just because you will see things and hear things at a level that he does not. When you sense there is something he should be aware of that can affect his performance, it is good if you have already established the ability to talk about business matters in a direct manner. Equally, sometimes he may want to tell you about some project he is working on that others in the company do not as yet know about; he wants your help in performing the task, and needs to know that you will keep it confidential. Here again, a direct relationship of openness about the nature of your work— established right at the beginning—makes it much easier later on to trust each other with important business matters.

A WORD OF CAUTION

It almost goes without saying that you must like and respect your boss. This does not mean you have to like everything about him or raise the level of respect to adoration. But unless you basically like and respect the person you work for, there is nothing but trouble ahead for both of you. The primary function of your job is to help your boss do his job better. He, in turn, must develop confidence in you and your abilities so that he trusts you with his work (which is also his career). Unless there is a feeling of mutual respect and confidence, things just will not work out well for either of you. If you have given the job a reasonable try but the feeling of comfortable interdependence is not there, I suggest you seek a change to another boss or another company.

TIP

Unless you basically like and respect the person you work for, there is nothing but trouble ahead for both of you.

LEARN THE COMPANY

Next to establishing a relationship of openness and mutual expectations with your boss at an early stage, the most important first task is to learn the primary business of the company and how the company carries out that business. Professional management analysts call the main business of a company its "mission." This mission may be expressed in a single sentence, or it may take several paragraphs. Your boss has a specific job in the company to enable it to achieve its mission. His work is the company's work; and the better he achieves part of the company's mission, the more responsibilities he will be given to achieve more of the company's mission. His work cannot be separated from the company's goals.

There are a number of practical ways you can find out what the company is about:

1. Ask for literature produced by the company that describes its mission and achievements, as well as its plans for the future. Annual reports provide a clear summary, as do employee brochures and magazine articles about the company. If you have a couple of weeks after being hired but before starting your job, ask your new boss-to-be or the company's personnel director for any literature that can help orient you to the company.

2. Ask your boss soon after you start working for him to tell you what the company is all about—its history, its structure, its mission, its policies, and its future. Not only does he know a great deal about it, but it is essential that you see it through his eyes. As you learn more about the company through working there, you may not always see it as he sees it; but it is still vital that you understand how he sees it in order to support him in his work.

3. Talk with others over coffee breaks and at lunch about their understanding of the mission and purpose of the company. The lower in the company's organization you talk, the more limited will be the perspectives of the person, so sift out what is important. Yet, you will learn things from fellow employees about what really guides the company that are not written down in the more formal mission and policy statements.

4. From time to time, ask someone outside the company—often someone who does business with the company—what he thinks the purpose and nature of the company are. This person will undoubtedly not know as much as you do about the company, but sometimes you get so close to it that it helps to hear someone comment who is not as personally involved.

5. And as you do your own work for your boss, ask yourself from time to time how this particular task relates to the company's overall mission. When you do this, you may understand more than you did before about what the company is trying to do, and certainly you will understand more how your boss's work contributes to the company's goals.

> **TIP**
>
> The mission is *what* the company does; policies and procedures are *how* the company goes about doing it.

POLICIES AND PROCEDURES

As you develop a rather comprehensive understanding of the mission of the company, you should also grow in your grasp of the company's policies and procedures. The mission is *what* the company does; policies and procedures are *how* the company goes about doing it. In many companies there are written lists of policies and procedures. Sometimes these are updated from time to time. However, two kinds of policies and procedures are not included in any written compilation: those that have been adopted since the last publication; and those that form the all-important "unwritten" policies that everyone who has worked within the company for a long time understands and operates by, but that cannot be found in any personnel memo or brochure.

Every organization develops its own personality, its own ways of doing things, its own system of unofficial rewards and punishments, its own standards of assessment of good and bad performance, its own network of people who really get things done regardless of who the official organization chart shows is responsible for a task. As a person who now needs to play an active role in making things happen on behalf of your boss (rather than take only a passive role in which you are merely told what to do and when),

you need to learn how to do things in the company way—according to both the formally stated policies and procedures and the unwritten ones that really govern how things work from day to day.

Unwritten Policies and Procedures

You learn the unwritten policies and procedures by asking your boss how to go about accomplishing a certain task, who to see, and when to see them. You should also ask some of the people who have been around the company for a while and who are on a more or less equal level with you.

Your Workplace Network

In time you will learn who makes up the effective working network. It may not turn out to be the same people your boss first thinks of, since he will tend to think at a higher corporate level than is really appropriate for your working level. You will, in essence, develop a network among the secretaries just as he has developed a network among the executives. Each network is a good one to help accomplish tasks; the choice of the right network depends on the nature of the task to be done.

> **TIP**
>
> Your overall loyalty must be to the company; your immediate loyalty must be to your boss.

LEARN YOUR BOSS'S JOB

And equally essential, you need to learn everything you can about your boss's job. He is responsible for certain kinds of work. This work might use a technical and professional vocabulary. You need to become familiar with this specialized vocabulary, to have a good idea of the processes or steps implied in these terms, and to have an understanding of how their use fits in with your boss's responsibility. There will be many times when he is out of the office or is not readily available and someone will call about a letter or memo he wrote, asking for clarification or further elaboration. The more you know about what your boss does, the better you will be able to provide correct and timely information if he cannot do so immediately. Where you are not absolutely certain about any information you provide in his absence, you should make that clear to a visitor or caller, indicate that you will refer the matter to your boss for confirmation when he returns, and leave the boss a brief memo about the matter. That way he knows what you've done and can decide whether any further steps are needed. Also he will not be surprised when the caller later refers to his conversation with you about the matter.

Ask the Boss

You can learn about your boss's job by asking him when you come across something new you don't understand, by reading books and magazine articles he can recommend to you, and by seeking out information on your own from the company or public library. Do not expect to become an overnight expert, but steadily increase your familiarity with the nature of the job you are helping him to perform.

Ask Other People

You need also to learn about the people with whom he deals. Some are in the company; others are outside—vendors, customers, consultants, professional associates, and colleagues in the same general line of work. He will give you information about who's who. You should quickly learn which callers are put through to him instantly and who he can more easily call back. Your caller will also give you (sometimes) a clue to the urgency of the call.

Study the Files

One of the best—and most essential—ways of beginning right at the start to learn about the company, your boss's role in the company, and who he does a lot of business with both inside and outside the company is to read the files of his correspondence. Start with the most recent and work backward. Not only is this an excellent way to learn this information, but it also helps you learn how the files are set up and gives you an overall familiarity with the range of business they cover. Right from the beginning your boss will ask you for certain files. "Bring me the file" is a request a secretary hears more often than any other. When you pull that file, glance through it so you have some idea about the history of the situation, and therefore you will have a better understanding of what is going on at the present and what will be taking place in the days ahead. Make sure that everything is in the file that should be there. The file becomes the written record of a series of transactions, developments, problems, achievements, and relationships. You will develop your own ongoing mental file of the situation that is contained in the formal file; but it is the best available record to refresh your memory and your boss's memory about the situation. Learn your files from the beginning.

TIP

The best response to gossip is to ignore it. Determine right from the beginning to gain a reputation as a nongossiper.

LOYALTY, GOSSIP, AND DRESS

Some personal matters are sufficiently important to be considered right at the beginning of your work as a secretary. These are loyalty, gossip, and dress.

Office Politics and Loyalty

Every continuing group of people develops a political character. Your office is no exception. Your boss is a part of the political process in getting things done in the company. He responds in certain ways to his superiors, to those who work under his direct supervision, those whom he must influence but cannot control, and those who make up the rest of the executive and staff work force in the company. "Politics" in this sense is not a negative word; it simply describes the fact that people have to learn how best to relate to each other to accomplish a common purpose, while at the same time meeting as best they can their own personal needs for recognition and advancement.

In any political environment, the participants are called on for loyalty to the cause and to the leaders. Because there are other players in the game besides your boss, there are many centers of loyalty in a company. Although your overall loyalty must be to the company, your immediate loyalty must be to your boss. Your efforts should be directed to helping him do his work in the best possible manner, to alert him to any problems you sense, and to suggest ways in which you can relieve him of routine chores so that he can devote himself

more completely to his professional and executive tasks.

Loyalty is a two-way street. As you continue to demonstrate your loyalty to your boss, he will most likely reciprocate in kind. As he moves around or up in the company, you could well move with him, since he appreciates loyal and competent support. Or he can assure that your future in the company is advanced (since he will speak well of you to others, including the personnel officer), even though he may not be able to take you along as his secretary when he goes to his new assignment.

Gossip

Wherever people continue in an ongoing relationship, talk is inevitable. Talk can readily become gossip. In every office, there are always some who love to gossip. "Gossip" in this sense is defined as idle talk, usually of a personal nature about others, often focused on rumors and speculation, generally of a negative, critical nature rather than positive and supportive. You might be the object of gossip; so, too, might your boss. The best response to gossip is to ignore it. Get busy with something else when you are invited to participate in gossip, say nothing about your boss, and become known as one who is not interested in the gossip mill. Offices all have nongossipers as well as gossipers, who are accepted for what they are. Just determine right from the beginning to gain a reputation as a

---

TIP

Basic knowledge about your company, your boss's job, the people he regularly deals with—an attitude of loyalty, a determination to be a nongossiper, and a pleasing, appropriate appearance: These are assets of great value. With them, you are well on the way to being a successful secretary.

---

nongossiper. Your boss will soon enough learn that you have not joined the gossip clique, and this will reinforce his loyalty to you.

Your Appearance and Dress

Loyalty and handling gossip is a matter of attitude; how you look is a reflection of you as an individual. Few companies these days have what used to be called a ''dress code.'' Even though there may be no rules about what you should wear or how much makeup/perfume or after-shave lotion you should wear, your common sense should give you some helpful leads. Your appearance tells others what you think about yourself. If you dress sloppily, others will readily come to the conclusion that you are a sloppy person in your work and in your confidences. Both you and your boss will be hurt by such a perception. Styles of dress vary from region to region in the country, from industry to industry within a region, and from office to office within a company.

What is appropriate dress for a secretary of a new junior executive on the third floor may not be at all appropriate for the president's secretary in the executive suite. Avoid drawing attention to yourself by either overdressing or underdressing in a bizarre manner. Understate your clothes, but with classical choice. Your appearance will then say to your boss, his bosses, and your coworkers that you are a professional who is focused on doing the job well. It's advisable to save your ''fun'' clothes for afterhour entertainment. You can certainly dress up to the level of importance in your company that is appropriate to the level of responsibility held by your boss.

Basic knowledge about your company, your boss's job, the people he regularly deals with—an attitude of loyalty, a determination to be a nongossiper, and a pleasing, appropriate appearance: These are assets of great value. With them, you are well on the way to being a successful secretary.

PART II
WITH THE OUTSIDE WORLD

One whole set of your secretarial relationships is with the outside world. Outside the company, that is. In some of these relationships you are an extension or agent of your boss. In others you are the sole contact that a person will have with your company or with your boss. In some you handle routine affairs; in others you can make or break your company's future with an outside person or firm.

Part II focuses on the range of relationships you have with people outside of your company.

CHAPTER 2
TELEPHONE

The telephone will be your main contact with people outside your own immediate office—whether with people who are outside the company or who are in other departments and sections of the company. This is true whether the calls are incoming—people seeking you or your boss—or outgoing—placing calls for your boss or making inquiries on her behalf.

TELEPHONE MANNER

Your telephone technique and manner give the caller a picture of the kind of person you are, the kind of person your boss is, and the style of office you both run. In fact, for many callers those telephone calls are the only personal relationship that the callers have with you and your boss. The impression gained from how those calls are handled directly affects business relationships with your company.

Pleasant and Unhurried Manner

Perhaps the most important contribution you can make is a pleasant and unhurried manner on the telephone. No matter how rushed and hassled you are when the telephone rings, stop what you are doing, wait for one more ring while you take a breath and compose yourself, and then answer the phone in a mood of pleasant helpfulness. You don't want to give the caller the impression that his call is an imposition. He should not bear the brunt of any hassle you might be experiencing at the moment. Another benefit from pausing for that moment is that your voice will automatically lower in tone. If you're tense, your voice is higher and more strident, less pleasant for the caller.

TIP

Your telephone technique and manner give the caller a picture of the kind of person you are, the kind of person your boss is, and the style of office you both run.

ANSWERING THE TELEPHONE

Your boss may have a particular way she wants the phone to be answered. Ask if that is so. If not, a satisfactory way of answering the phone is (if your boss's name is Miss Smith):

"Good morning (afternoon). This is Miss Smith's office. Jane (John) Dow speaking. May I help you?" This answer achieves several things right at the beginning. It creates an initial cordial relationship: "Good morning" is more personal and courteous than a mere "Hello?" It identifies the office immediately to the caller; if the switchboard has plugged in a call for Mr. Jones to your extension by mistake, the caller can correct the matter without taking any more of your (or his) time. And it lets the caller know that Jane (John) Dow is ready to assist him, and he can start in at once to explain why he is calling. Try to use the caller's name at least once in the conversation; by doing so you are confirming that you got it right and you always flatter someone when you use his name.

TELEPHONE MESSAGES

If he asks to talk to Miss Smith, there are now several possible scenarios that can occur:

Miss Smith is out of town and will not be back in the office until next Monday. You need not explain to the caller whether Miss Smith is on business, where she is, or whether she is on vacation. Miss Smith's private and business affairs are not a matter for general conversation over the phone. Ask for the caller's name, telephone number, and reason for wanting to talk with Miss Smith, and indicate that Miss Smith will return the call after she returns. Perhaps the easiest method of getting all the needed information in a convenient form for your boss is to use one of the prepared telephone message pads. One form manufactured by the 3M Company has a slightly adhesive edge that makes it easy to stick to even a vertical surface. Other forms have similar spaces for information, but without the adhesive edging. These telephone message pads are readily available in stationery and in office-supply stores; your own supply department may buy them in bulk.

Note the information that the form guides you to secure: name of the person to whom the message is directed (normally your boss); date and time; name of the person from whom the message comes; his company and phone number; whether he called or came personally; who is to call whom next; whether the matter is urgent; any short message to be given to your boss; and the name or initial of who took the call, so your boss may ask any follow-up question before returning the call.

TIP

The most important contribution you can make is a pleasant and unhurried manner on the telephone.

Having this information about a number of calls that came in while she was out and who they were from gives your boss some choice in setting priorities on returning the calls. She can also ask for files and other information before placing a call, ensuring that she has all the information she needs before she calls. Among these calls may be some from her boss and from customers or clients you know to be very important, or calls about issues you know are critical at the moment, or calls that the caller stresses to you are very urgent and have to be returned as soon as possible. If the caller has to be called by a certain day or time, be sure to highlight that information for your boss.

IF YOUR BOSS IS AWAY

If your boss is away from the office for several days, the pile of little telephone-message notes might be more confusing and create more clutter than is desired. You can then type up a list of calls by day, using columns for the information:

Calls on February 7, 1992

From   Phone   Comments

You can place in the comments column any particular information about calling back or messages given to you for your boss. This system organizes all her February 7 calls for her to scan through on her return and allows her to take whatever action she needs to in the light of all the other matters she must attend to after an absence. There should be similar sheets of paper for her February 8 and February 9 calls.

INTERRUPTING YOUR BOSS FOR A CALL

Some executives have you take information on all incoming calls—except those from her boss—and then every couple of hours or twice a day will set aside time to return calls that came in during the day. These executives have chosen not to have their work interrupted constantly by incoming calls. If she chooses to use the telephone this way—and I think it gives her better control over what she wants to do with her day—you should tell the caller that Miss Smith is not available at the present time, but she will return the call later that morning (afternoon). If the caller is traveling and will not have ready access to a telephone, get the best available number for the next day or two. Most calls are not so earthshaking in content that another day or so is critical. If the caller insists that he has to talk with your boss this very day, ask him to wait a minute and say you'll find out whether Miss Smith is now free, put him on hold, and give your boss the message. If your boss still does not want to talk to the caller at the moment, apologize to the caller, saying how very sorry you are that Miss Smith is not available to receive his call at the moment. It is then up to the caller to leave a telephone number or state that he will call again later.

If a Visitor Is in Your Boss's Office

If your boss is seeing a visitor in her office, there is little that is more irksome and discourteous to the visitor than your boss receiving a continual flow of incoming calls while the visitor waits to complete a sentence. Work out with your boss which kinds of calls are urgent enough to interrupt if there is a visitor in the office.

TIP

Develop a list of regularly called telephone numbers.

MAKING OUTGOING CALLS

You will also have to make outgoing calls, sometimes placing a call for your boss, sometimes making a call yourself in relation to some office matter. You should develop a list of regularly called telephone numbers. This will save time and frustration in having to look up numbers constantly or having to call information for a number. Where possible, secure the direct-dialing number, thus saving time having to wait while your call is serviced through a central switchboard. List these numbers in a card index system, one in which cards can be readily entered or discarded. Depending on the nature of your relationship with the person, name, company, and telephone number are must items; mailing addresses may be useful; other information such as spouse's name, children's names, special professional or personal interests may be useful at times if your boss wants to use this kind

of information in her dealings with the person. Some bosses like to make a letter or call sound more personal by asking to be remembered to a wife or husband (and if the person's spouse's name is on the index card to remind your boss, she's more likely to use the right name).

When you place a call for your boss, it makes a splendid impression to ask the person you are calling (or his secretary) "Are you (Is Mr. Jones) free to accept a call from Miss Smith at this time?" This accomplishes several things at once: It establishes that Miss Smith is calling; it flatters Mr. Jones in that it assumes he may be too busy right now to take Miss Smith's call; it also flatters him by giving him the choice of taking the call; it allows him time to get papers or documentation together before calling Miss Smith back. Normally, you'll get right through.

THE TELEPHONE POWER GAME

Some executives play a power game on who places calls and who answers the telephone first. Other executives like to receive and place their own calls directly unless they are busy in meetings or have visitors. You will

soon learn which is which. This question, "Are you free to accept a call from . . . ," tends to blunt the force of the power game by its gentle courtesy.

"IS HE IN?"

Until you get to be on good speaking terms with an answering secretary, avoid asking "Is he in?" when the phone is answered. This friendly shortcut works well with frequently

made calls when you and the answering secretary are on good terms, but it is rude when tried with someone you seldom call.

When placing a call on an office matter,

say, "This is (your name), calling for Miss Smith of ABC Company." Then ask for the information you want. This formula quickly identifies who you are, what company you are calling for, and who your boss is. The identification of your boss's name is necessary only when the call is on her behalf and her name is the key to secure the data or action you are seeking. Sometimes you may need to refer to her title or responsibility in the company in order to get the action or response you need. By giving this information, you allow the person taking the call to know the level of responsibility in your company that he is dealing with.

"I'LL TRANSFER YOU"

When trying to place a call to a person who holds a certain specific responsibility in a large company, you may end up being shunted from one office to another. Keep a scrap-paper listing of the number of transfers; after four or five, feel free to get indignant and to let the next person who answers know that she is now the sixth person you have talked to trying to find out where to find your information. That will tend to focus attention on getting you to the proper party more quickly. And keep this experience in mind when someone is being shunted around in your telephone system; ask for the information required and tell the caller that the right party will call back. Then find out who in your company should make the call and pass the request to that person. To that caller *you* are the ABC Company. Since you know your company better than an outsider does, you should ensure that the right person in your company is located, rather than passing the caller on to a seemingly endless succession of transfers.

GET THE NUMBER RIGHT

When you take down telephone numbers, repeat the number to ensure you have it right. It is frustrating to your boss when she is returning a call and the number you gave her is not the right number. In like manner, when you give your number for someone to call back, repeat it yourself if the other person does not repeat it back to you.

ENDING A CALL

Always close a telephone conversation with a pleasant word. "Have a good day" is trite; so is "Take care." "Thank you so much for your help" is fine; so is "It's such a pleasure to find someone so helpful." Even "Goodbye, Mr. Jones" is excellent, since Mr. Jones has heard his name used in a pleasant manner. If the caller or the person who answers your call hangs up with the feeling of "that was nice," your next call will be welcomed. Even if you are calling about an unpleasant matter, you can convey a personable manner in dealing with it. Such a manner will generally get more accomplished and help to maintain more relationships than will angry confrontation. If there has to be confrontation, it is better for your boss to handle the matter.

"HELLO"

If you are placing a call and someone answers "Hello," ask if this is the XYZ Company or Mr. Jones's office. By doing that you can quickly make sure you've got the number you are seeking.

"I'LL PUT YOU ON HOLD"

If you answer a call and need to put the person on hold, ask first if that is satisfactory or does the person want a callback. Often the caller is calling from a long distance and does not want to wait holding a dead telephone line without even being given the option of doing so. If the caller is on hold and it begins to look as though your boss will not be able to get to the phone soon, get back to the caller and explain the situation, suggesting that your boss will call back soon. Sometimes the person on hold has decided not to wait any longer or has had something arise that forces him to hang up. If you know who it is, try to have his call returned as soon as possible. If you don't know who it is, but the person soon places the call again, try to put the person through without further waiting.

CHAPTER 3
RECEPTION

Depending on the size and organization of your company, there may be a receptionist who presides over a lobby or reception area to welcome visitors from outside the company. This receptionist usually serves as an initial screen: securing the visitor's name, company, purpose of visit, person to be visited, and calls you with that information if the person wants to see your boss.

KINDS OF VISITS

Several conditions may now apply:

A Previously Made Appointment

1. The person has made a previous appointment and is expected. The visitor may be an old friend of your boss's or may be a stranger. This then may be a first visit or one of a long series. Your boss may be free to see the person right on time, or something unexpected may have come up that results in the person having to wait.

What you do depends on whether your boss is free right away. If so, you will normally tell your boss that his expected visitor is in the waiting room and ask whether you should go get him. If the visitor can be seen at once, you let the receptionist know that you are coming right away to the reception room. If the visitor will have to wait a while, let the receptionist know about how long that might be. Although the visitor naturally prefers to be ushered in promptly to see the person with whom he has

---

TIP

Your own "company reputation" grows according to how you treat your visitors as well as on how you support your boss.

an appointment, it is always courteous—and good for the relationship—to keep him informed about the length of any unexpected wait.

Who goes to get the visitor depends on who the visitor is and how your boss likes to manage such matters. Normally you will go to the reception room, ask for the visitor by name, identify yourself, and guide the person to the office. You would show him into the office, simply announcing his presence if he's an old friend or introducing him if he's a first-time visitor. If, however, the visitor is a VIP or an old friend (or both), your boss may want to go to the reception room personally to welcome this guest. If that happens, you should smile and say hello as the two pass your desk. If you already know the person, this renews your personal acquaintance; if this is a new visitor, you may well have occasion to speak to him on the phone in the future and this initial pleasantness makes the future relationship easier for both of you.

In some instances, you may be working in an office where there is no separate receptionist or waiting room. In this case, you have to combine several functions in quick succession. You first have to ascertain who the visitor is, determine whether the visitor is known to your boss, find out if your boss is free (or desirous) to see him, put the visitor at ease while waiting, take any coats that need hanging up, and inform the visitor how long he might have to wait if there is a delay. In such a situation, the waiting area is often close to your desk, so you have to continue with your own work while being watched by the visitor for any clues about when he can see your boss. You need to blend a friendly personableness with an official reserve, so you can do your work without shutting the visitor out as though he were an inconvenience. You never know how important any visitor will be to your company's business, so always try to make his welcome and wait as pleasant as possible. It sometimes helps to put yourself in his position and to think of the Golden Rule: Treat each visitor with as much thoughtfulness and courtesy as you would like to be treated.

No Previously Made Appointment

2. The visitor does not have an appointment. In such a case, he may be an old friend of your executive's who is dropping in on the off chance that they can spend a few minutes together. Or the visitor may be a salesperson who is trying to break into your boss's day, hoping to make a sale. Or it could be someone with an idea that could change the nature of your company. The receptionist will give you the initial information that the visitor first makes known. You then have to do some quick investigation and decision-making. What more can you find out about this visitor and what he wants with your boss? Does your boss know him or want to see him? If the visitor is known and your boss does not want to see him, you will have to turn him away with graceful regrets. You may never see him again; but then again he may become very important to the company. You may forget him, but he will not forget the manner in which he was denied access to your boss. Again, put yourself in his place. Tell him that your boss is not free to see him today; or that the company already secures services from a vendor with whom they are very happy and that the company is not considering change at the present; or that your boss would very much like to see him at a mutually convenient time and could the visitor please call to confirm an appointment in three weeks; or your boss likes to see initial proposals in writing before making appointments, so could he please write a letter with a summary of the proposition he wishes your boss to look at before an appointment is made.

If the visitor is someone who has pestered your boss, you can explain to him how busy your boss is, that this is not a good time to even say "hello," and is there any message he would like to leave? Even though the person goes away without having accomplished his mission—which was to see your boss—he should go away with the feeling that he had been considered to be important as an individual, that he has been listened to, and that his concern will be expressed to your boss. Tact and a touch of diplomacy keep your boss's special place of esteem in the eyes of this kind of visitor while at the same time preserving your boss's time and privacy.

The Visitor is Early

3. The visitor is early. Not just five minutes early, but thirty-five minutes early. In such a case, your boss may be just as happy to see him and get the appointment over with that much sooner. If that is the situation, the only problem you have is knowing how this change of schedule will affect the succeeding events in your boss's day.

If, however, your boss cannot see the visitor until the appointed time, you may have to suggest a convenient way of filling in some time. If the visitor has work or reading he has brought with him, there is little need to help him fill in the time. Otherwise, you may ask him if he would like to see the latest copy of some magazine (popular, news, or trade) which you have in the office. Or you might get him a copy of the morning newspaper, if there is one around. Or you might offer him a cup of coffee while he waits. There is no real obligation that you do any of these things, since he is the one who has arrived early and has created the problem. Still, if you can suggest something to fill in his time, if there are no reading materials in the waiting area, you

can be assured he will be most appreciative. And he will most probably make some comment to your boss about how helpful you were.

Your Boss is Running Behind Schedule

4. Your boss is running late and cannot see the visitor for thirty minutes. Now the shoe is on the other foot and you do have some obligation to mollify his feelings. Your boss will apologize when he sees him, but if you can offer a kind of peace offering in the form of a cup of coffee and the latest issue of the trade magazine that covers your business, the apology will be readily accepted and their meeting will not have to overcome the caller's initial barrier of hurt feelings or resentment at being considered secondary to some other demand.

The Visitor is Late

5. Your visitor is thirty minutes late and rushes in with a breathless word of frustration at traffic delays. At the same time, your boss has a full day of appointments that will be affected in some way by this delay. First of all, you should put your visitor at ease and accept his explanation at face value, sympathize with him about the problems of getting about at this hour, and tell him you will let your boss know he has arrived. There is nothing like having a couple of minutes to collect yourself after rushing without being able to catch up.

You may then suggest—as you usher the visitor toward your boss's office—that your boss (Mr. Smith) has a very full day and you know Mr. Smith will be grateful if the visitor could keep in mind that Mr. Smith's next appointment is in forty-five minutes. By doing this, you have tactfully given the visitor a schedule within which to conduct his business with your boss.

CONFIRM THE APPOINTMENT

Some secretaries find it useful to call people who have appointments with their boss the day before the appointment just to confirm that it is still on the visitor's schedule. This practice achieves several things: It reminds the visitor that your boss takes his appointment schedule seriously and is busy enough to need this confirmation; it tends to flatter the visitor that your boss should think so highly of him as to confirm the reservation; it sometimes unearths the fact that the appointment was forgotten (which the visitor would probably not admit to you) or that it is no longer possible due to schedule conflicts that have since arisen or that it is no longer needed due to the changing business situation. The net result is a smoother day for your boss and a pleased business colleague who was called the day before his scheduled appointment. These calls may take fifteen to thirty minutes during the day, but they are well worth the effort if your boss has a tight schedule.

You may choose to limit such calls to people who, you have learned, tend to forget or run late. But interestingly, the ones who appreciate such a call the most are the ones who normally don't need to be called. What they appreciate is being thought of; they also will admire your efficiency.

WHO MAKES THE APPOINTMENT

Some people will call to make an appointment with your boss. Some executives make their own appointments; some want you to make routine appointments for them, reserving the option to veto such an appointment. You need to work out with your boss the appointment system he wants to adopt. If you do have the responsibility of making some appointments for him, you should always do so tentatively and tell the person who wants the appointment that you will confirm it after you clear it with your boss. You might suggest that you need to check with his calendar. You can then reschedule the appointment when you confirm it; or you can cancel it altogether if your boss does not want to see this person.

KEEPING THE
MASTER APPOINTMENT CALENDAR

In any case, every day you should update your appointment calendar with his so that you are both expecting the same people at the same time. If your boss has been running his own appointment-reception service, this may take a little tactful training of him on your part. But the end result will be a smoother life for him and a much more controlled life for you. The management of his appointment and reception service is an important way you can take a great load off his shoulders, enabling him to give his time and energy to his work instead of trying to control his visitors as well as do his work. You may have to point out the benefit of this to him before he turns this over to you in full, but once he's done it, he'll never want it back.

COMPANY VISITORS

Another kind of visitor is someone from another department in the company. Some will call ahead to make an appointment to see your boss, others will just wander by and want a quick word with him. Depending on the nature of the relationship with your boss—and the person's position in the company—he may feel free to stick his head in your boss's door and interrupt him without giving it a second thought. He might just want a short discussion of some problem or to tell your boss the latest joke making the rounds. Or the person may be a junior executive who stands in some awe of your boss, wants to see him on some matter of importance, or just wants to make a positive impression and be remembered. This last type of company visitor will more likely go through you to set up an appointment.

Regardless of which kind of company visitor wants to see your boss, you should treat him pleasantly and helpfully. Your own "company reputation" grows according to how you treat your visitors as well as how you support your boss. People in the company will begin to hear about you often before you actually meet them, and much of what they hear will be based on comments made by company visitors to your boss.

If your boss is busy or out of his office when a company visitor drops by, be sure to make a note of the visit and any comments regarding the purpose of the visit. The effectiveness of your boss's work in the company often is based on snippets of information about plans, problems, and people that drop his way quite casually. His company visitors are an indispensable source of such bits of information. And part of your job is to help keep the flow of information coming his way by helping his company visitors feel at ease when coming to see him. Your boss will let you know which company visitors are to be discouraged.

A TACTFUL GUARDIAN OF THE DOOR

Acting as the guardian of the door to the office is a responsibility that calls for sensitivity and judgment. Some secretaries are possessive: They think they always know what is best for their boss and do their best to protect him from interruptions they don't approve of. Whereas they may think they are keeping him from "just another salesman," they may, in fact, be turning away an invaluable new service or major new idea that would be of great help to your company. People from outside the company will accept being turned aside from presenting their proposal if your boss has heard them enough to grasp what they propose and then explains that now is not the time or conditions are not right to consider the matter further. They at least have the sense that they have been heard before being told "no." But they will become highly dissatisfied if they get the feeling that a secretary has preempted the boss's role and has decided that their proposal will never even be placed before the boss for consideration. Although they would prefer to talk to the boss directly, there is less dissatisfaction if you carefully take down the particulars of their proposal, place it before your boss, and later call back to relay his decision not to see them or not to proceed further with the matter. They at least feel that their proposal—in however garbled a form when compared with how they themselves would have presented it—was considered by your boss and not blocked by his secretary.

A NOTE ABOUT OUT-OF-TOWN VISITORS

Often people who are visiting your city or town for a day or two on business try to set up several appointments during their visit. They will try to establish the most important ones first; by "most important" I mean those that are already linked with present business and are aimed to maintain or increase that business. When those are established, they will try to build appointments for new prospects around the times already committed. Your boss might be on the "old business" list or the "prospect" list. Both are important to the visitor—and may be important to your boss. Business is built on an ever-increasing circle of acquaintances and knowledge of related businesses.

CHAPTER 4
CORRESPONDENCE

Correspondence flows in two directions: from outside your office to your boss and from your boss to those outside your office. Some of the letters your boss writes originate with her; some are part of or develop into an ongoing correspondence for which a large file grows; and some are replies to letters sent to her.

INCOMING CORRESPONDENCE

Companies and bosses vary on how incoming mail is handled. Generally the mail is first delivered to a central mail room where it is sorted by floor and office. During the day someone from the mail room makes two or three deliveries of mail that has accumulated for your office. This mail includes both letters from outside correspondents and interoffice letters and memos.

In some companies all mail addressed to the company is opened in the mail room. If there are checks or money orders enclosed, they are separated, accounted for, banked, and their amount and purpose noted. The letters are then sent to the appropriate department for handling. In such a company, your boss's mail and any mail addressed to you or of a nature to be handled by your boss would come to your desk opened. In these companies, envelopes marked "Personal" or "Confidential" would probably arrive on your desk unopened by the mail room.

In most companies mail addressed to the company in general is opened in the mail room, but mail addressed to a particular person is not opened there, but is sent directly to that person for opening. In this case, all letters addressed to your boss or you would arrive on your desk unopened; and letters addressed to the company that the mail-room people think are your boss's responsibility to handle would arrive opened.

You and your boss must agree on how she wants you to prepare her mail. First of all, you must determine how to recognize personal mail from business mail. She may receive certain private business mailings at the office that she alone wants to handle. She has to tell you which firms or people might send her personal mail; those letters you should place on her desk unopened and in their own pile.

She will generally want you to open all her business mail. You both should decide whether mail marked "Personal" or "Confidential" includes you or not. Much depends in answering this question on the nature of the business and your boss's role within the business. You can expect increasingly to be a confidant in most of her business life—with the possible exception of certain personnel matters and possible future reorganizational matters. But even in these, you will be increasingly trusted to handle this kind of information in its developmental stages as your relationship with your boss grows in mutual trust.

When you have opened the mail, organize it into three or four categories. Discuss with your boss how many categories she wants. Among the possible categories are:

1. Urgent: These are letters that require immediate attention. Her response to these letters might be to dictate an answer at once, to start an investigation for further information, or to call the person. You will soon learn which letters are really urgent and which are merely important.

If you separate the urgent letters from others, she can at least focus on the former if she has only a short time in the office between meetings or appointments.

2. The important letters that she will have to answer herself, but which are less than urgent.

3. The   need - to - read - but - no - action - required letters: Much of an executive's career is based on having timely information about her business, her company, her colleagues, her competitors, and trends in her field. Many people will send her mailings or copies of correspondence which do not require her per-

sonal action, but which are part of the context in which she has to work and make decisions.

4. Magazines, journals, newspapers, monographs, and the like: There are general-interest magazines and newpapers (*Time* or *The Wall Street Journal,* for instance), trade or professional publications, and technical monographs and books. She may wish to leaf through these for whatever information she can quickly glean, or she may wish to study some particular subject in great detail. She can guide you in evaluating the importance she places on the various kinds of printed material that cross your desk.

5. Special reports and studies: From time to time she may be on a committee or task force that requires the reading or preparation of special reports or studies. These reports can often be quickly perused, but sometimes call for intensive study prior to a meeting. Timing and the nature of your boss's connection with the project will sometimes require that these reports are in her urgent pile and sometimes in her "will read, if possible" pile.

Before you place the correspondence on her desk, there are several steps you can take. These should be discussed with her so you are both agreed on your taking these steps:

1. Highlight the subject matter or action requested. Use a colored underline or highlighter. This will draw her attention at once to the main point of the letter. She can read the rest of it if it is a matter that directly concerns her, or she can decide that it is of incidental interest to her and not spend any more time on the letter.

2. Get the file, if this is part of an ongoing correspondence, and send the letter and file in together. This will save having to get it later; it will enable your boss to answer the letter in the light of what both parties have said in the past.

TIP

As you grow in familiarity with the job and in a working relationship with your boss, there are many matters that you will be able to handle on your own, but for her.

3. Use a date stamp and date-stamp the letter when you first process it. It is sometimes more important to know when you received the letter than when the writer dated it.

A CORRESPONDENCE LIST

If your boss is away for several days, it is helpful for her to have her mail more thoroughly organized for her attention on her return. For instance, all her urgent mail should be in a single folder. Then a folder can be prepared for each day's "important but not urgent" mail, with a short summary of the person, company, and subject matter typed on a sheet that is attached to the cover of the folder. All of the "to read" mail can be in a single folder, as can the printed magazines and newspapers.

By doing this, it will be much easier for her to care for urgent and important correspondence as quickly as needed, while the background information and general reading can wait their turn in her schedule.

MARKING THE LETTER

It is a useful practice if you both agree to use a particular color pen or pencil for marking a letter. Your underlining or highlighting or any notes you might make on the letter should always be in the same color. Hers should be in another—and consistent—color. Many executives merely check a corner in that color to indicate that they have seen the letter. If she does this, both of you know that an unmarked letter means an unread letter; this is often a useful thing to know when trying to reconstruct a file or a sequence of actions.

Any notes she makes on the letter asking you to secure more information should be made in "her color" pen or pencil. Any notes you jot down in response should be made in your color. This practice makes the flow of information very quick and obvious, without having to spend time trying to figure out who made which notations.

TIP

Many routine matters might, in time, be handled in your name rather than hers. Don't grasp for this responsibility too quickly, but don't wait indefinitely for your boss to suggest that you do what it seems obvious you can do perfectly well.

```
┌─────────────────────────────────────────────┐
│                    TIP                        │
│                                               │
│  Keep an index file for people and firms with │
│  whom you regularly correspond, and list      │
│  their zip codes in the file.                 │
└─────────────────────────────────────────────┘
```

MATTERS YOU CAN HANDLE

As you grow in familiarity with the job and in a working relationship with your boss, there are many matters that you will be able to handle on your own, but for her. You can separate these letters; research the matter in the files, if need be; and write an appropriate response for your boss's signature. When you place this before her for signature, you should include the original letter for her to glance over. By doing this, you not only take over a more or less routine task, but you also keep her fully informed so she is never surprised should she meet the writer sometime outside the office and the contents of her letter are mentioned.

Again, depending on the nature of the business and on your relationship with your boss, many of these routine matters might, in time, be handled in your name rather than hers; and incoming correspondence relating to them would begin to be addressed to you. My advice is don't grasp for this responsibility too quickly, but don't wait indefinitely for your boss to suggest that you do what it seems obvious you can do perfectly well.

OUTGOING CORRESPONDENCE

Letter writing is a major part of a secretary's job. Many of those letters will originate with your boss. The form they take depends in part on her work patterns and the size of your company.

She may write out a draft letter in longhand. Your job then is to transcribe it on the typewriter or word processor. This method can take her longer than is most efficient for routine letters, but it may be the best way for her to think through a complex problem and get it carefully down on paper.

Perhaps you should type out the first draft of such a letter with double spacing so she can refine it before proceeding to the final single-spaced letter or report.

She may type out a draft letter herself— some executives like to have a typewriter by their desk. After she has refined her own first draft, then you type out the final letter or report.

She may dictate the letter. There was a time when all secretaries learned shorthand and executives dictated to the secretary face-to-face. Even though some system of shorthand or speed writing is useful at times, fewer secretaries learn this skill and fewer executives request it. Electronic dictating systems, some with portable dictating units and others with telephone-dictating access, have just about replaced the direct executive-to-secretary, dictation-by-shorthand method. Indeed, in many larger offices, routine transcription is now handled by a word-processing department that processes overnight the dictation that was telephoned in by dozens of executives. In such an office, you as a secretary are more likely to manage the flow of dictation between your boss and the word-processing department than to type out the correspondence yourself.

In smaller companies, your boss may have a dictating recorder she can take home or on a trip; you would have a transcribing unit that plays back her dictation tape through earphones or a speaker. Usually you control the playback with foot controls and type out or word-process her correspondence throughout the course of the day.

Your boss may be an expert dictator, or she may need your suggestions on improving her dictation. She should spell out new or unusual names or words. She should specify where she wants periods, paragraphs, or any special punctuation or indentation. She should learn to speak crisply—including consonants—and reasonably slowly. You can slow up the transcribing playback if she talks too quickly to understand readily, but that lowers the tone of her voice on the unit. With each tape or disk of dictation, she should return all the correspondence she used when dictating so you have a complete file and can refer to the original correspondence in determining proper names and addresses. Sometimes there is a paper tab which she can use to mark the length of correspondence—and even note which letters are to be given priority in processing. If she uses this tab system, you should ensure that her unit has a fresh supply of tabs before she takes it on an extensive business trip.

There was a time when secretaries had to type a letter perfectly on a manual typewriter, and since no one can do that constantly, the secretary had to learn how to erase the original with little or no mess—and up to four or five carbons. This was very time-consuming and not at all efficient. These days a secretary has a correcting electric typewriter (with either a lift-off correction tape or a cover-over correction tape) and a photocopy machine. The letter can be readily corrected line by line as it is typed and proofed while it is still in the typewriter. The photocopies are exact replicas of the original corrected final copy; no carbon copies need correcting. A secretary might have an electronic typewriter that holds the letter in memory; if mistakes are detected, they can be easily corrected without disturbing the rest of the text and a corrected final copy quickly run off. Increasingly more secretaries have word-processing systems that combine a display screen with a large memory. Here also corrections can readily be made and corrected final copies run off. In recent market studies, one major office-machine corporation has found it is selling nine correcting electric typewriters to every one electronic typewriter and ten electronic typewriters to every word processor, but that the ratio changes each year in favor of electronic typewriters and word processors.

The ogre of the perfect letter—and perfect carbons—does not present the problems it once did before the advent of the electronic office. Most word-processing programs even have spelling checks that can locate obvious typographical errors. These spelling checks do not pick up words that are spelled correctly but are the wrong words, such as "than" for "that" or "is" for "in." You still have to proof your letter for sense, even though your word-processing spelling check has found all your *teh*s and *fo*s.

Business letters these days are usually typed flush left—every line begins flush against the left-hand margin. There is also a minimum of punctuation at the end of lines. The reason for this goes beyond clean appearance; it is based on time and motion studies that focused on using the least number of keystrokes. Because each keystroke takes a fraction of a second and makes possible the introduction of another error, fewer keystrokes mean less time in typing a letter and less time in correcting a letter—hence, less cost in the overall preparation of the letter. For one or two letters, this may not seem to add up to much of a saving, but when multiplied by many thousands of letters across the years, the savings are substantial.

A standard flush-left letter has the following characteristics:

Date

The date is normally expressed as *December 12, 1989* with no punctuation other than the comma between the day and the year. In the military and many government offices, and increasingly in many corporations, the date is expressed as *12 December 1989* (as it is in most European countries) with no punctuation at all. In both cases, the month is fully spelled out. Abbreviations for months are considered informal and not suited for business correspondence. In some few offices and in many government agencies that use documents in scanned computer applications, the date is expressed in numbers only in the sequence of year-month-day and with all months and days expressed in two-digit figures. The computer can then sort dates easily. In this system, January 1, 1990 is expressed as 19900101; December 25, 1989 is 19891225. In a computer sort of these numbers, the earlier and later dates are easily put into chronological order; this is much more difficult for a computer to do when dates are expressed in the more standard ways.

Name, Title, Company, Address, City

The first line of the formal address is the name of the person to whom the letter is being sent. You may use the title of address, such as "Mr.," "Mrs.," "Miss," or "Ms." In some instances, you would use a title that is related to a position or profession, such as "Senator," "Congressman," "The Rev.," or "The Hon." Increasingly, however, these titles of address are not included in business letters. Here again keystrokes are saved; and the awkward decision of how to address a woman is postponed until the opening salutation.

When the person's company title is used, it is usually placed on the first line, separated from the person's name by a comma: Janice L. Resnick, President, or William T. Smith, Production Manager.

The second line is usually the company name, spelled out in full or with commonly advertised abbreviations. Abbreviations for businesses are considered an alternate (or sometimes primary) legal name for the company. Both "International Business Machines Corporation" and "IBM Corporation" are acceptable. In the interest of saving keystrokes, the abbreviations that are in common use without any periods should be typed accordingly ("IBM" not "I.B.M.").

The third line is the street address or box number. If there is a special floor or department, it is often used as the third line and the street or box as the fourth line.

The fourth line is the city, state, and zip. Because the post office is steadily proceeding toward optical scanning of addresses for sorting purposes, the two-letter post office abbre-

---

TIP

The language used in business correspondence is concrete, direct, to the point. It does not try to create literary effects or use much humor or wit. It is writing for the sake of conveying clear, unambiguous communication; it is not intended to be beautiful or memorable writing.

viations for the state are in general use: "MA" not "Mass.," "CT" not "Conn.," "CA" not "Calif.," and "NY" not "N.Y." Here again keystrokes are saved. You will soon learn the abbreviations for states you commonly send letters to, but you will need to keep a list of all fifty states in your desk for those times you send a letter to a state whose abbreviation has slipped your mind. You can obtain a list from the company mail room or the post office.

A fifth line may be used for another country.

The postal service wants all mail to have zip codes. It will not accept bulk mail or Express Mail unless the zip is part of the address. Normally you will be corresponding regularly with people so their zip code will be available to you from their correspondence. If you have much correspondence without such information, you should purchase a postal zip book (through your purchasing department). This book lists every zip code in the country, with street numbers in cities and towns that have more than one zip code.

Keep an index file for people and firms with whom you regularly correspond, and list their zip codes in the file.

SALUTATION

The opening word of greeting is called a salutation. In business correspondence it usually consists of the word "Dear" followed by the person's name: "Dear Bill," "Dear Mr. Smith," "Dear Ms. Adams," or "Dear Senator Brown." If you know a woman to be married or single, the appropriate "Mrs." or "Miss" is acceptable, although many businesswomen increasingly prefer "Ms." as a counterpart to the masculine "Mr." The salutation is followed by a colon in business correspondence and by a comma in informal correspondence.

There is a further problem when addressing a firm. Once "Dear Sir:" was standard; "Dear Sir/Madam:" used occasionally. Often the single word "Gentlemen:" was used. In these days when business-letter writers as well as book writers try to avoid sexist language, the easiest way to address a firm is to use the firm's name: "Dear RCA:" or "Dear Wagner & McCready." People at the firm will route the letter to the proper person to deal with your letter, regardless of the salutation you used.

On your index cards for addresses, note how your boss likes to call a person. Some are "Mr. Jones"; some are "Bob" when the formal name is "Robert," but some "Roberts" are called "Robert." And, some "Roberts" might even be "Bud" or some other nickname that is unrelated to their formal name. Use the formal name in the address and the more personal name in the salutation. Get your boss into the habit of mentioning which salutation she prefers when she dictates her letters. If she gives you a list of names and addresses for letters with identical contents to process, ask her to note how she wants the salutation for each letter.

BODY OF THE LETTER

Each paragraph of the letter starts with the first word flush to the left-hand margin. Paragraphs are separated by a line of space. It is generally good practice to restrict a letter to a single topic of business. There are several reasons for this: If the person to whom a multitopic letter is sent handles one of the topics, she may file the letter without having dealt with any of the other topics; it is difficult to know where to file a multitopic letter; cross-referencing such a letter in a filing system is costly and often unreliable. If your boss has five items she wants to write someone about, it is better to write five short letters—one on each point—than to write one long letter that covers all five points.

Each letter should normally consist of an opening paragraph. This paragraph should include reference to earlier correspondence or telephone calls and should indicate the subject about which the letter is being written.

The next paragraph or two should develop that subject, specifying any action that is requested or has taken place.

The final paragraph should conclude with any request or promise of future action or information.

CONCLUSION

Many business-letter writers close a letter with a standard phrase of conclusion such as "With every good wish," or "With all kind regards." This is a polite way of concluding a letter without seeming to close it abruptly and rudely. A comma normally follows this line; if your boss adds the words "I am" (With every good wish, I am) or "I remain" to the phrase, no punctuation follows the phrase.

COMPLIMENTARY CLOSING

This formal closing of the letter usually consists of "Sincerely," "Sincerely yours," or "Best wishes" in business letters. "Truly yours" and "Very truly yours" seem to have passed out of general use. This line, too, is followed by a coma.

Name

Leave about five lines for the signature and then type the full name. Many signatures are so stylized (that's another way of suggesting that many are illegible) that it is a service to the recipient to be able to see the name typed out. Five lines gives plenty of space for a large, flowing signature, yet a small, tight one is equally enhanced by the surrounding spaciousness.

If your boss uses letterhead with her name and title printed on the stationery, there is no need to type in her title after her name following the signature since that information is already provided. Indeed, some executives do not want their name typed after the signature, feeling that it is not needed since the name is printed. If, however, your boss uses general company stationery, both her name and title should be typed. The name line has no concluding punctuation, nor does the title line.

If you write a letter in your own name, you should normally use your boss's letterhead and write "Secretary to Miss Smith" on the line following your name on the name line.

DICTATOR/SECRETARY

It is normal to include the initials of the dictator and secretary. Sometimes only the initials of the secretary are typed, since the dictator's name is on the letter. If the dictator's initials are JDS and the secretary's are MFB, the pattern might be JDS/mfb or JDS:MFB or simply mfb.

```
┌─────────────────────────────────────────────────┐
│                      TIP                         │
│  Work should go to your boss as perfect as you   │
│  can ensure it; you should not try to slip away  │
│  from this responsibility by saying "it was      │
│  their fault."                                   │
└─────────────────────────────────────────────────┘
```

COPIES AND ENCLOSURES

It is normal to indicate to whom copies are sent and to list any enclosures. Once the abbreviation "CC" or "cc" was used for "carbon copies." This abbreviation continues in use, even though the copies are more likely to be photocopies. Increasingly, the word "Copies" is used, followed by a colon and the list of people receiving copies in alphabetical order. You would normally draw an arrow pointing to a name for the copy going to that person. Enclosures are indicated by "Encl" followed by a colon and the items enclosed.

The list of people to whom copies were sent is useful both to your boss and to those who receive the copies. Your boss will have a record for the future of who was sent a copy of the letter. Each one who receives a copy will know who else has the information contained in the letter. Sometimes a "blind copy" is sent to someone for special reasons. That person's name is not listed on the "Copies" list, but is listed as a "Blind copy" on your file copy and on the recipient's copy but not on the original. Your boss will thus know she sent a blind copy, and the person receiving the copy will know that others do not know that he has the information.

Enclosures are listed for two reasons: You will know from your file copy what other material was included in the original mailing; the person receiving the mailing will know if anything he was supposed to have received was inadvertently left out.

A standard business letter will look like this:

March 28, 1989

Richard C. Brown, DP Manager
ABC Company, Inc.
123 Fourth Street
Des Moines, IA 45678

Dear Mr. Brown:

This is further to our telephone conversation this morning about a Destruct-All shredder.

We would be pleased to provide you with a demonstration shredder for two weeks' use with no obligation. You can test its effectiveness and thoroughness in your actual working situation.

Mr. Robert B. Tompkins, our Midwestern representative, will call you early next week to set up a convenient time to install the demonstration model and to review our sales terms. If you decide to purchase a Destruct-All shredder, we can deliver your new shredder at the same time we pick up the demonstrator.

Thank you for looking to us, and with every hope we can be of complete service to you, I remain

Sincerely yours,

John D. Smith
Sales Manager

mfb

Copy: Robert B. Tompkins
Encl: Destruct-All booklet

The language used in business correspondence is concrete, direct, to the point. It does not try to create literary effects or use much humor or wit. It is writing for the sake of conveying clear, unambiguous communication—often with a stranger; it is not intended to be beautiful or memorable writing. It tends to be more impersonal than personal, more correct than idiomatic, more formal than informal, friendly but businesslike.

Sometimes your boss will add a personal paragraph at the close of a business letter to deepen a personal relationship or friendship that has grown out of the business relationship. In fact, there is a level of relationship that can develop in which a business letter would be considered rude and even hostile by the receiver if those personal notes were missing. In such letters, your boss may use more direct language—less stilted business-type language—than she would in a letter to a stranger.

Such a letter might look like this:

December 2, 1989
Robert S. Williams
XUY Company
987 Sixth Avenue
Atlanta, GA 34567

Dear Rob:

I think it's time to come up with a new focus in our advertising campaign. We're increasingly disappointed with the number of orders and dollar amounts drawn from the ads in the trade journals.

Perhaps we need to zero in on more narrowly targeted markets, rather than to major so much on general corporate promotion. Think through our products and the specific markets that they appeal to. Can you come up with some suggestions of who make up specific demographically identifiable markets of at least 250,000 people by the time we have our next regular meeting in March?

We're depending on you for a breakthrough in this.

Give my warmest regards to Meg, and remind her that we all have a date at the top of Peachtree on me since I lost that bet on the Falcons.

As always,

Sincerely,

John D. Smith

HANDWRITTEN CORRESPONDENCE

Sometimes in the interest of saving time and typing costs, a boss might respond to an inquiry with a handwritten note. This note might be written on the sender's original letter, which is returned to him as his answer. You keep a photocopy, of course, for your record. Another method is to use a memo pad that has carbons or noncarbon copies as a part of the pad. In this method, you send the original and keep a copy for your files. Usually this approach is used when the message is short, the topic is transient (of short-range importance), speed is important, and the person is known to your boss.

It is of interest to note that studies show a typewritten business letter costs nearly eight dollars to produce. This includes such factors as your boss's time, your time, and machine costs, as well as postage and stationery. Little wonder then that some bosses will dash off a handwritten note from time to time.

PRESENTATION FOR SIGNATURE

If you type or word-process the correspondence yourself, be sure to proof it carefully before sending it in for signature. Watch especially for dropped words, and for such easy-to-make but hard-to-detect errors as "in" where you should have an "is." If you have an electronic typewriter or word processor, be sure not to erase the letter until you have proofed it, run out the final copy, and have had your boss sign it. There is always the chance that she will make some minor alteration at the last minute.

If she has an urgent letter she wants to send out by some Express-Mail method, take the letter in to her to sign as soon as you have completed it. Otherwise, take batches of letters in for signature two or three times a day. A safe and systematic method is to place the letter—signature page on top if the letter runs more than a single page—in the flap of the envelope. When you pick up the signed correspondence, you need only ensure that the letter is signed and that the right envelope is used for the letter. Everything is right there for you to fold and place in the outgoing mail tray or the mailbox.

Once the letter is signed—thus making sure there are no last-minute changes—the copy goes into the file for possible future reference.

If you assign your boss's correspondence to a typing pool or a word-processing department, be sure to proof it before sending it in for her signature. Even though someone else has proofed it earlier, that person may not know just how a certain word is spelled, may mistype a name, or may simply have missed an error. The work should go to your boss as perfect as you can ensure it; you should not try to slip away from this responsibility by saying "it was their fault." If you become known by the word-processing department as a stickler for perfection, they will accept the fact that you are doing your job well and will proof all the more carefully any work they do for you.

ACCURACY

When typing a business letter—whether for your boss or writing it yourself on her behalf—check and double-check for accuracy. There are several matters to be especially careful about;

Names: No one likes to see his or her name misspelled.

Addresses: Company names and zip codes need close attention.

Figures: It is so easy to transpose numbers or leave a decimal point out.

Dates: In calling a meeting or reporting on one, it is important to get dates and times correct. Double-check days and dates. For instance, if you use "Friday, March 12, 1988," check to make sure that the

Friday you refer to is indeed March 12. If you miss on either the day or date—for example, if Thursday is really March 12—the reader might show up on the wrong day.

General spelling: When in the least doubt, look it up. It is quicker to use a "speller-divider" book than a dictionary. Excellent speller-dividers are easily available in bookstores and office-supply stores.

Hyphenation: If you use hyphenation to avoid very short lines in a letter, check the right place to break the word, again using a speller-divider or dictionary. American-style hyphenation is based on how the word is pronounced, whereas British-style hyphenation is based on the roots of the word. The American system hyphenates "democracy" after the first *c: democ-racy;* the British follows the pattern of hyphenating according to derivation: *demos* (the common people) + *cracy* (rule by), hence the hyphenation *demo-cracy.* Your American-produced dictionary and speller-divider follow the American usage, but don't think your British correspondents are uninformed if they hyphenate slightly differently.

The problem of just where to hyphenate can get especially tricky when you use a word in different forms. For instance, "philosopher" is hyphenated as *phi-los-o-pher,* but "philosophic" is *phil-o-soph-ic*—all because the accent has shifted. Likewise, the verb "present" is hyphenated *pre-sent;* the noun "present" is *pres-ent.* If you have the least question in your mind, look it up.

Your letter is all the recipient may ever see of your company, your boss, or yourself—so make sure it is a first-class and accurate picture that you send.

Usage changes steadily, so do not depend on patterns you learned years ago. And refer to recently published usage books, rather than earlier—and now outdated—editions. Not only do you want to be regarded as accurate, you do not want to be considered old-fashioned. There is, for instance, a growing trend to use fewer and fewer commas in correspondence. "Correct" style is based on thoughtful application of present usage more than on mechanical obedience to certain rules. For instance, in times past the following sentence would be punctuated fully in this way:

In 1980, the stockholders met in Chicago, Illinois, on March 17. This year, they will meet in the same city and on the same date, too.

Today these sentences are more likely to be typed:

In 1980 the stockholders met in Chicago, Illinois on March 17. This year they will meet in the same city and on the same date too.

The overall appearance is cleaner, and there is no confusion of meaning with the commas left out. If, however, confusion might result without a comma, by all means put it in.

A useful set of the following books by your desk will enable you to solve most questions of accuracy and usage that may arise:

a college-level dictionary (better than a short paperback version)

a speller-divider

a usage and style manual

an almanac

a concise encyclopedia

CHAPTER 5
RESERVATIONS

Sometimes business associates will visit your company for an extended visit, for a two- or three-day meeting, or as a party on tour. Your boss may have the responsibility of serving as their official host. As part of that task, arrangements have to be made for travel, dining, hotels, meetings, and sometimes entertainment. It may be that your boss has an extended trip for which travel and hotel arrangements need to be made.

One facet of your job is to organize all the arrangements initially and then make last-minute changes as people arrive unexpectedly, fail to arrive, or change their minds at the last moment.

TRAVEL

Today most business people travel by air. If you handle a great deal of air travel, you should encourage your boss to subscribe to the *Official Airlines Guide* (OAG). There is a North American edition and an international edition. These guides list all scheduled flights by all airlines, together with connecting flights where more than one plane or airline has to be taken from point to point.

If you depend solely on an airline-reservation system for information, there is a tendency for them to favor their own system even though some other airline might offer more convenient flight times or routes and lower prices. Your ability to find your way around

the OAG will at least enable you to ask good questions about alternative flights and routes.

If you depend solely on a travel agent, you usually will get excellent service. Each agency is tied in with one of the major airline-reservation systems for its up-to-the-minute information. Your agent is generally better prepared to know the state of the business so he too can ask the right questions about alternative flights and routes, and especially better prices. However, it doesn't hurt if he knows you are reasonably knowledgeable and are looking at alternatives. It will help to keep him alert to the very best arrangement for you, and not to take your request for granted and present the first solution that comes to his computer screen without exploring further.

Since airline deregulation came into effect, pricing has become competitive. (There was a time when the Federal Aviation Administration set the fare structure for every route; airlines had to compete in the area of services and style since fares were standard.) Now that fares are flexible, prices for a particular flight can change almost daily. And there are several different prices for seats on the same plane. Even travel agents cannot keep up with all the available rates and with the constant changes in the rates. You have to ask the agent to find you the best rate available; and he in turn has to get that information from the airlines on a need-to-know basis.

Since deregulation new airlines have quickly come into being. Most of them offer lower rates and/or more elaborate services in an effort to attract customers who have not heard of them before. Most travel agents will tend to think only of the older, more established airlines they have long been familiar with. You can help by reminding them of these newer lines from time to time. You can find out which of these newer airlines serve your community by glancing through their ads in the travel or business section of your local newspaper.

If your boss and his associates do a great deal of travel, there are a few travel clubs that send listings of current air-travel bargains. These clubs usually have a toll-free telephone number and will serve as a travel agent. Their annual membership fee is expensive, but their specialty is finding seats for their members at the best available rates. In some instances, they may even recommend buying a through ticket, but getting off at an intermediate stop. For instance, your boss may want to travel from Philadelphia to Fort Worth. A Philadelphia-Los Angeles ticket with a change of planes at the Dallas/Fort Worth Airport might be several hundred dollars cheaper than a direct Philadelphia-Dallas/Fort Worth ticket. So your boss would buy a Philadelphia-Los Angeles ticket and merely deplane at Dallas/Fort Worth, not using his Dallas/Fort Worth-Los Angeles segment. The only thing to bear in mind for such a flight is his need to take only carry-on luggage; he could not check his luggage only to Dallas/Forth Worth under normal circumstances. That special Philadelphia-Los Angeles via Dallas/Fort Worth rate may be operable only for a three-week period and only on certain days of the week. You could spend hours trying to find this information; your travel agent would probably not be aware of it; the airline would not suggest this possibility; only a travel club committed to searching out such possibilities in the ever-changing rate picture would know. Advertisements about such clubs appear in airlines' inflight magazines and in travel magazines and magazines for frequent flyers.

The easiest way to purchase tickets once you have determined which flight is best—or have presented the options to your boss and gotten his decision—is to have an account with a local travel agent. The agency will prepare the tickets, deliver them to your office in time for the flight, and bill your company. An alternative is for your boss to use a standard credit card, pick up the tickets at the counter on the day of his flight, and put the bill on his expense account. If it is given sufficient advance booking time, an airline will mail tickets that are charged over the telephone to your boss's credit card. The disadvantage of his picking the tickets up at the counter at the time of the flight is a possible shortage of time. He may be running late in getting to the airport and there might be a line for ticketing that is both aggravating and could cause him to miss his flight. All too often the person just in front has a long, complex flight schedule to consider with an equally complex ticket to write up while the minutes tick by. A late arrival can also result in getting a poor seat because the better seats may have already been assigned to other passengers.

Many airlines permit advance seat reservations and will also send advance boarding passes. With these in hand, your boss need only present his ticket at the boarding gate, check whatever luggage he wants checked with the redcap at the curb, and board the plane. These advance seat reservations and boarding passes are possible for both legs of a round-trip flight. Smaller airlines tend not to provide these services.

RECONFIRMATIONS

If you have visitors from overseas, their flights will have to be reconfirmed at least 72 hours before they are scheduled. Reconfirmation is not always required for flights that originate and terminate in North America. But for any ticket purchased abroad, reconfirmation must be made on all flights that originate in North America, whether they are bound for another North American destination or for an overseas destination.

Ask your overseas visitors for their tickets (often two or three books of tickets stapled together). Have them tell you whether they want to make a flight change or whether they will stay with their plans as ticketed. Then call the airline for the next flight at least 72 hours prior to that flight and tell them that your visitor is still planning to take the flight as ticketed.

If there are changes to be made, the best place to call to get them taken care of is an office of the airline that first issued the ticket. The next best place is the airline the visitor wants to fly on next.

If you have a group of visitors, your travel agent might be willing to take all the information—and the tickets—from you and make all the needed changes and reconfirmations for you. However, you should burden your travel agent with this chore only if your overall travel purchases warrant such an imposition on his time and equipment.

As much as possible, find out from your visitors where in the aircraft they like to sit, including smoking or nonsmoking areas. Without promising them results, tell them you'll try to see that the airline accommodates their desires.

VIP AIRLINE CLUBS

Most major airlines have private clubs for VIPs. In the early days of commercial flight, membership in these clubs was by invitation only. In recent years, membership is by payment; with only a few airlines retaining the idea of membership by special invitation. Membership can be annual or for a larger fee lifetime. They usually include membership privileges for the member's spouse. The airline club issues membership cards, which have to be presented at the club for admission.

The club provides a quiet, well-appointed place to wait for departure. A receptionist will handle seat reservations and any last-minute travel needs (apart from actual ticketing). Free

coffee and tea are available, sometimes free fruit juice and breakfast rolls; and free local telephones. There is a bar that, depending on the airline, may be free or may charge a small amount for drinks. Some clubs offer a small conference room for business conferences.

Depending on your company, your boss may have an airline VIP club membership paid by the company as a benefit if he travels constantly, or he may wish to join one or more on his own. If he is a member of such a club, there is usually a private reservation number for club members. Travel-reservation requests handled through these special numbers are usually given special attention.

TIP

Many airlines permit advance seat reservations and will also send advance boarding passes. With these in hand, your boss need only present his ticket at the boarding gate, check whatever luggage he wants checked at the curb, and board the plane.

FREQUENT-FLYER PROGRAMS

Many major airlines have a special promotion program for frequent flyers. If your boss has reason to travel often on the same airlines, he might well join these frequent-flyer programs. He is issued a card and a frequent-flyer number. Whenever reservations are made on that airline, the frequent-flyer number should be given to the airline's reservation representative. This means that your boss will be credited with mileage for the flight when he completes it. On some flights bonus mileage is given at times.

Numerous benefits are available for him to select from as he reaches various mileage levels. These include free upgrading to first class, free car rentals, free hotel rooms, free flights, and the like.

Sometimes the frequent-flyer program has a special reservation number also.

MEALS

Your visitors may have special food requests. Someone may want a Kosher meal; another a vegetarian meal; and a third a salt-free meal. Although it is not widely advertised by the airlines, they will make every effort to provide a passenger with special meals given enough advance notice.

When you get preliminary flight information from your visitors, include a question about any special diet wishes as a matter of course. If there are any, you can let the airline know at the same time that you make the reservation or the reconfirmation.

RENTAL CARS

Ask your boss whether he uses one of the "big three"—Hertz, Avis, or National, or one of the smaller, sometimes less expensive rental agencies. Your company may have an account with one of the companies. If that is the case, your company probably gets a discount on each rental.

Your company probably has a policy on whether full insurance is to be taken out each time a car is rented, whether such insurance is covered by a company insurance policy, or whether the company self-insures such coverage. Information about the type of car desired, your boss's driver's-license number, insurance preferences, and discount percentages are fed into a central computer if your boss holds a car-rental frequent-user card or credit card.

Car-rental reservations should be made at the same time flight reservations are. By using the car-rental frequent-user number or credit-card number, the filled-out forms will be waiting for your boss when he arrives at the airport. Otherwise, he will have to wait for a reservations representative at the counter to fill out all the information. Each major car-rental company has a toll-free telephone number for making reservations.

HOTELS

Your boss may have favorite hotels in different cities he visits on business. He will certainly let you know which these are and ask you to make reservations there when he goes to a particular city. Or he may have favorite hotel systems he uses when possible. If he stays regularly at hotels that are part of a national or international system, call the system to see if they have a hotel in the city he is to visit. If so, make the reservation. If not, check with his second-choice hotel system.

When you make a reservation, you will have to call the hotel directly if it is an independent; or you can use a toll-free number if it is part of a large system. Reservations are normally held until 6 p.m. If your boss may arrive after 6 p.m., you will have to guarantee payment. This is normally done by giving the hotel his credit-card number. When payment is guaranteed, the hotel will hold his room overnight and will charge his credit-card account even if he fails to arrive. If payment has been guaranteed at a hotel and his travel plans have changed, be sure to call the hotel to cancel the reservation prior to 6 p.m. of the day in question.

Several hotel systems have frequent-traveler programs. Cards and numbers are issued; sometimes a slightly higher fee is charged for "tower suites" reserved for club members. Often rooms are upgraded at no extra cost, and local newspapers are delivered to the room without charge. If your boss is a member of such a program, reservations should be made through the program's special-reservations number when he stays at one of their hotels.

RESTAURANTS

Your boss may have to entertain a dozen visitors who are attending a meeting at your company over a three-day period. He may decide to throw a party for them one evening at a fine local restaurant, and you are to make the arrangements.

First, decide with him where the party is to be held. Then call the restaurant and ask to talk with the manager or owner, depending on the size and nature of the establishment. Explain that Mr. Smith is entertaining guests and wants them to have an outstanding time. Therefore he has chosen the Bon Appetit Restaurant. You might need to go over to the restaurant, choose with the manager an appropriate table, and select with the manager the right menu and wine. Set up an appointment for the visit.

When you are there, select a quiet corner—far from the kitchen, the entrance, and the bus stands—where tables can be put together to accommodate the party. If possible, meet the waiter or waitress who will handle the meal and express your appreciation for all the care you know your party will receive.

You may be able to select the menu yourself, depending on how well you know the restaurant, its offerings, and your party. Or you may wish to take a copy of the menu to your boss, with the recommendations of the manager. Are all the meals to be the same? Or is each person to order separately? Much depends on how quickly the party is to be served, and whether some further activity follows the meal. Seek the manager's advice about the chef's specialties for such a group, even though it may not be listed on the menu. And make arrangements about paying the check, including all tips. Payment could be made with your boss's credit card, by company check, or by billing the company directly. Small restaurants will want payment on the day of the meal, since they have to keep tight control of their cash flow; larger restaurants may be quite pleased to bill your company, hoping for further business in the future. There should be little problem with a restaurant with whom your company regularly does business.

Inform your guests that the meal is at a certain time, say 7 p.m. Plan with the manager to start serving at about 7:30 p.m. This will give latecomers time to settle in. People can have drinks while arriving and relaxing. If all your guests are staying at the same hotel, and if the restaurant is some distance away, you may have to arrange with the hotel manager or concierge for taxis to deliver them and pick them up. If your guests plan to arrive at the restaurant from various locations, be sure to give them clear directions, including the restaurant's telephone number on a typed card or piece of paper. When you are at the restaurant making preliminary arrangements, you might pick up enough of the restaurant's business cards or matchbooks for each of your guests. Having the card or the matchbook will at least refresh their memory on where they are to be or enable them to have a taxi take them there.

If there is an event after the meal, be sure to tell the restaurant manager so he can ensure that the meal is finished at the proper time. Here again you may have to make taxi or car-service arrangements to transport your group from the restaurant to the office, the hotel, the theater, or wherever the event is held.

If it is wintertime and overcoats need checking, it is easier to make arrangements for the coatroom attendant to handle the coats as a group—with payment to be made as part of the restaurant's total bill—than for each guest to deal individually with the coatroom attendant.

If you are there for the meal, you should quietly keep track of time and services and bring your needs to the manager's attention, when necessary. The more successful you have preplanned and arranged for the party, the less noticed your stage-managing will be. Even though you get involved in conversation with one or more of the guests, keep one eye and ear on how things are going, trying to anticipate any problem in time to mention your concern to the manager. If, on the other hand, you are not there for the meal, go over all the arrangements you have made with your boss. Give him a short list of those arrangements so he will know what you have done and what to expect.

A SMALL BUSINESS LUNCH

Your boss may frequently ask you to call a nearby restaurant to make lunch reservations for an office visitor and himself. He may specify the restaurant; he may ask you to find a free table at the last moment in one of three or four restaurants he normally patronizes. If he is well known at the restaurant, getting a good table is easy. Your reservation request goes something like this: "Mr. Smith has an unexpected and important visitor he'd like to take to lunch at Antoine's. Can he get a quiet corner table in half an hour?'' When Mr. Smith arrives, he will be greeted by name and cared for at once; his guest will be suitably impressed.

If you are calling a restaurant where Mr. Smith is not known, your reservation request may go something like this: ''I am calling for Mr. Smith of ABC Company. He has an unexpected and important visitor that he wants to take special care of. That's why I'm calling Antoine's. Can he have a quiet corner table in half an hour?'' Since Mr. Smith is not a regular there, he may not get the corner table, but he'll get the best available table—and again his name will be recognized.

Sometimes your boss may ask you to take a visitor to lunch since he is not available to do so but wants to extend this courtesy to the visitor. Unless you are also known at the restaurant, it may be best to make the reservation in your boss's name, indicating that you are bringing one of his special visitors to lunch. You will probably be expected to pick up the check. Use your boss's account or his credit card, or make arrangements to get enough petty cash before you leave. Get a receipt, including tip, so you can make the required report to the accounting department. Ask your boss to give you clues about what the visitor enjoys talking about. Follow those clues by asking questions and listening with care to learn something new. Every talker knows when he has a good listener. And listening carefully to your boss's visitors is always far safer than talking about him and the company.

ENTERTAINMENT

From time to time your boss may want to provide entertainment for his out-of-town visitors: theater, concerts, sporting events, and other special activities. The company may have several season tickets, for instance, to home games of a local professional or college team. If so, he might prefer to give the tickets personally to his visitor. Your boss may or may not go with his guest. You may be asked to have the tickets delivered to the visitor's hotel with instructions on how to get to the stadium or arena.

Or you may be asked to make reservations and get tickets for some event in town. There are two very helpful sources to go to. One is a ticket agency. They charge a small fee for each ticket they secure, but they are likely to have the right contacts to get the best available seats or seats for a sold-out performance. Ticket agencies are often located in first-class hotels; if your guest is staying at a hotel where there is a ticket agency, use that one. The other source is the concierge at your visitor's hotel, if the hotel has one. A concierge is a very knowledgeable arranger. All world-class European hotels have a concierge; many hotels that cater to business people in America are adding concierges to their staffs. The job of the concierge is to ease the guest's way in the city.

Before making seat reservations for concerts or the theater, you might want to ask your visitors where in the house they like to sit. Some prefer the balcony, some the orchestra. Without promising a particular location, explain that you will try to arrange for tickets as close to their preference as possible.

Because of the lateness of these arrangements at times, you may wish to have the ticket agency deliver the tickets to your guest's hotel rather than to the office.

If there is a party of several, the earlier the reservations are made, the more likely you will be able to secure a block of seats. In general, a block of seats three or four wide but two or three rows deep is preferable to a long line across a single row. It keeps your party together as a unit.

Tickets should be given to each member of the party ahead of time, either at the restaurant if they are eating together or in their hotel message box. If you wait until arrival at the theater or arena to distribute tickets, someone is sure to be missing or late. Someone will have to wait outside for that person.

If your boss has a business trip to a city where there is an activity he would like to attend—from opera to boxing—and he has

asked you to make some arrangements, you can call the front desk of his hotel there and ask whether they have a concierge. If so, ask the concierge to make the arrangements for your boss. If there is no concierge, ask for the name and telephone number of the ticket agent with whom they do the most business. Call the agent for information and reservations.

It is not unusual for excellent seats to be available at the last minute; it is not wise, however, to count on them turning up.

CHAPTER 6

EXPRESS SERVICES

Most of your contact with out-of-town people will be by regular mail or by telephone. Either the matter is so urgent that a telephone call is required; or there is no rush, in which case an extra day or two in mail delivery makes no significant difference.

Since a business letter costs nearly eight dollars, sometimes it is less expensive and much easier to make a two- or three-minute telephone call to clear up a matter. However, your boss will usually want a letter written if the matter requires a record. She will even dictate a confirmation letter that follows up the telephone conversation if she wants the matter on record.

Sometimes you will have to send a letter or package that absolutely *has* to reach the recipient that very day or early the next day. You now need to use the right express service.

MESSENGER

Messengers deliver letters and parcels in a citywide area. Your company may be large enough to employ someone who serves as a messenger when needed. It is more usual, however, to use a messenger service. Your company may have an account with one of the messenger services in town. You either call the service directly with your request, or you ask whoever coordinates messenger services in your company to provide the service you need.

If the package has to arrive by a specific time—rather than just in the "late morning" or "early afternoon"—you need to make that clear when you place your order. Since messengers usually try to batch deliveries and pickups by areas of the city—delivering and picking up at several locations in the same vicinity—any special-priority package needs to be specifically identified.

COURIERS

In larger cities, there are courier services that can arrange for hand delivery of packages to other cities or to overseas cities. Your company will be required to pay the air fare—or

---

TIP

Sometimes you will have to send a letter or package that absolutely *has* to reach the recipient that very day or early the next day. You now need to use the right express service.

---

part of the air fare, if the courier is delivering on behalf of several companies—and the courier service fee.

Courier services are normally used only when the package is of exceptional value or importance. Courier services can be located in the yellow pages of the telephone directory or through reference by a district traffic office of a major airline.

EXPRESS MAIL

The U.S. Postal Service offers an overnight Express Mail service. Rates are the same to any location in the country and are based on the weight of the package. There are two rate schedules: one for delivery to the recipient's location; a lower one for delivery to a post office location. If your recipient uses a post office box for mail delivery, the lower rate is just as quick, since the post office normally does not deliver Express Mail to the business or home address of post office box holders.

Before sending Express Mail, you need to check with the post office about a number of variables:

1. Does the Postal Service offer Express Mail service to the zip-code location you have addressed the package?

2. What is the cutoff time for you to deliver the package to your post office for overnight delivery to be guaranteed?

3. If you want Saturday or Sunday delivery, are they available at your recipient's location?

One major disadvantage of Express Mail is that you have to deliver the package to the post office in order to get it into the system. Although the Postal Service delivers Express Mail, unless you are a post office box holder, it does not pick Express Mail up from your office. However, your office mail room might handle this.

UNITED PARCEL SERVICE

The largest national parcel-delivery service is United Parcel Service. UPS makes arrangements for both pickup and delivery. Unless your company has a regular account with UPS and is on a daily pickup schedule, a fee is charged for pickups each week they are made. This fee is added to the delivery charges for the first pickup of each week in which pickups are requested. Arrangements for pickup can be made by using a UPS toll-free telephone number. Pickup normally occurs the day following the call in which the pickup order is placed. You need to find out from your UPS operations center the latest time you can call in for next-day pickup.

UPS has entered the guaranteed overnight air-express delivery service. Its rates, as of the time of writing, are excellent for larger, heavier packages and less competitive for letter-type deliveries. UPS, again at the time of writing, serves fewer locations than some of the other overnight air-express services. Since this is a rapidly developing service, you will have to keep abreast of rates and locations served regularly.

OVERNIGHT AIR-EXPRESS SERVICE

There are a growing number of overnight air-express services. The two oldest and best know are Federal Express and Purolator Courier, with Airborne coming on quickly. These express services arrange for both pickup and delivery, using toll-free telephone numbers for pickup arrangements or service inquiries.

Normally you can call in as late as 4 p.m. for same-day pickup and next-day delivery. The time may vary forward or backward a bit, depending on your location. These companies have radios in their delivery vans and require their drivers to call in regularly, so last-minute pickups are part of their service.

These companies run their own fleets of airplanes, which converge at a single location during the night with all the packages collected by the vans during the day. Overnight the packages are sorted and sent back to regional distribution centers, from which they are carried by van to the delivery addresses. Thus, a package sent from Los Angeles to San Francisco is likely to go overnight from LA to Memphis. There it is put on the San Francisco plane and delivered by van midmorning the next day.

Most of these companies provide their own mailers and boxes to make it easier for you to package an express delivery for them. They also provide airbills (forms that include your name and address, account number to be charged, your recipient's name and address, and delivery instructions). If you establish an account with the air-express company, they will provide you with a supply of airbills with your account number, your business's name, and your address preprinted on the forms. You need fill in only the sections relating to the recipient and shipping instructions. A copy of the final airbill that contains the charges for the delivery is enclosed in your statement from the express company so you can pass on express charges to a customer, as appropriate.

Each express service publishes a regular listing of zip-code areas served and notes any unusual extra services possible or limited services, as appropriate. When you call the toll-free number for a pickup, you are asked for your account number. The operator enters this into a computer, which instantly provides your name, address, and particulars of locations (2nd floor, for instance, and time of closing). The operator will confirm with you that these particulars are still in effect. Then the operator will give you a confirmation number, such as "NZW 95." This means that you are customer number 95 for the NZW route for the day. If there is a breakdown in

---

TIP

Each express service publishes a regular listing of zip-code areas served and notes any unusual extra services possible or limited services, as appropriate.

pickup arrangements, you use this confirmation number when you call the company's toll-free number to find out why the pickup has not been made by the time you expected it.

When the driver picks up the package, you will be given a copy of the airbill. Use the airbill number to trace the whereabouts of any package that did not arrive when you expected it to do so. Perhaps as many as five percent of the packages may be lost or delayed, often due to adverse weather conditions. The airbill numbers are recorded at each stage of delivery: from the van to the distribution center, from the distribution center to the central-sorting center, from the central-sorting center to the addressee's distribution center, from that distribution center to the van, and from the van to your company. Within minutes of your call to the toll-free number, you can know who last handled the package and whether it is on the van that serves your recipient. Since these companies are in fierce competition with each other, the percentage of packages misrouted or delivered later than midday is continually being reduced.

These services offer guaranteed overnight or priority delivery for a premium rate. They also offer standard air-delivery rates, which guarantee two-day delivery, and usually provide overnight delivery. These rates are about half of the guaranteed overnight delivery rates. If a couple of days is good enough—much better than a week or more by parcel post—use the standard rate.

INTERNATIONAL

Both the U.S. Postal Service and the air-express services offer deliveries to overseas addresses. Depending on the nature of the package, expect some delays for customs clearance. And remember that some countries are more efficient in releasing packages from customs than others.

Always let your recipient know that such a package has been sent, with airbill or Express Mail number, so arrangements can be made at the receiving end to speed up release from the authorities.

AIRLINES

Airlines offer package and letter (parcel) service. This often means you have to make arrangements for the package to be delivered to the airline counter or cargo office at the airport; and your recipient has to make arrangements to have it picked up at the airport of destination.

This option does mean, however, that a particularly crucial package can be delivered by you at the end of a business day to the airlines at the airport, flown to the city of destination, and picked up there on arrival. The cost is usually less than an overnight air-express service since you and your recipient are serving as your own delivery and pickup services.

Airlines serving overseas locations also offer package and parcel service, but here arrangements may have to be made for customs clearance through a customs brokerage company. An airline normally uses a company of its own choosing when the sender has not specifically named one. Unless your recipient knows how to utilize such a company—which also charges standard fees for paperwork, which are high for a small package of relatively little value—it is more convenient for

your recipient if you use International Express Mail or one of the air-express services.

TELEGRAMS AND ELECTRONIC MAIL

There was a time when Western Union (WU) dominated the overnight (or faster) express message market. WU offered almost instant telegraphic service from office to office, slightly longer service when using a messenger (including the famous "singing telegram"), and overnight service in what was called a "night letter."

With deregulation of the communications utilities and the advent of new technologies, the Western Union telegram is no longer the only option available for short messages or money orders. Western Union's services are more likely to be found in the form of franchised agencies that handle telegrams and money orders as a part-time extra business than in the form of WU offices in every town and neighborhood. And deliveries are more likely to be by telephone with a mailed confirmation copy of the message than by a uniformed messenger. But call your nearest WU office to find out the nature of the services available for rapid message transmittal.

Radio Corporation of America (RCA) handles a wide range of overseas message traffic. If your community has an RCA office, find out the nature of their services.

The Postal Service provides overnight electronic mail. Services vary depending on the location of both the sending and receiving locations. Since these services are growing rapidly, find out the current state of services from your local post office. Electronic mail is a message sent from one computer to another—often by satellite, or else by telephone or radio transmission—printed out by the receiving computer on a message form and delivered by the Postal Service. Since many advertisers use

electronic mail, an urgent message delivered by electronic mail sometimes does not convey the same sense of urgency that a Western Union night letter once did.

When originating telegrams, overseas cables, or Postal Service electronic mail, you have to get the message to the transmitting company. Often this can be done over the telephone, with the charge for the service eventually showing up on your telephone bill. Sometimes you can have an account with the transmitting company and receive a monthly statement for messages sent during the previous month. Or you may have to take the message physically to the transmitting company's office and pay for the cost of its transmittal then and there.

A growing alternative for larger companies for interoffice mail handling is internal electronic mail. Computers—mainframe, minicomputers, microcomputers, word processors, personal computers, and the like—are connected to each other by "communications." They can send messages back and forth either in a batch during day or night or at the actual time of the communication, permitting people at either end to type out short messages to each other. A normal way for electronic mail to be sent in a computer-integrated company (one office in San Francisco is "integrated" with the New York office by a communications hookup between computers) is for messages to be sent over a telephone line from computer to computer during the night. First thing in the morning, you or your boss can call up on your screen any messages that were sent in during the night. You can get a hard-copy printout of these messages if you wish, and file and send any replies for communication back to the originating office. If your office has—or enters—this integrated, electronic office system, you will receive instructions on how to operate it for your own firm's electronic mail.

The message is no different from what it would normally be when using paper. You compose it or read it on a screen; you "open" it by pressing a couple of keys. It is just a little harder to say "It must have been lost in the mail."

CHAPTER 7

INTERNATIONAL CORRESPONDENCE

Your boss may have regular correspondence with overseas companies or colleagues. In general, correspondence with people overseas calls for the same basic rules as all business correspondence: one topic per letter with clear, direct, concrete language. However, a number of special points should be kept in mind when handling both incoming and outgoing overseas correspondence.

Much depends on how well the overseas correspondent knows English—and on which kind of English he knows—and whether his English is a second language, and what his native language is. Each of these factors determines how he uses English, how well he understands English, and whether his English presents any unusual characteristics that you should keep in mind.

CHARACTERISTICS OF LANGUAGE USE

Sending and Receiving

Every user of a language is both a sender and receiver. You normally understand many more words that you hear or read than you normally use in your own speech or writing. You recognize them or guess their meaning close enough, even though you may not use them as a working word in your everyday vocabulary. This is true also of grammatical forms. You have a feeling for when grammar is correct and when it is less formal, even though you may have forgotten all the special names for verb forms or all the rules for dealing with gerunds. And usually we are more at home with our spoken language than with written language.

Levels of Formality

We use our language at different levels of formality. A person who is speaking to the annual meeting of a company's stockholders uses a different level of vocabulary and grammar than when telling a joke at a backyard barbecue. A person who is interviewing for a job uses a different level of formal language than when describing the interview to a close friend.

Levels of Education

There is educated language, that is, language used in formal and informal situations by a person who has had years of formal education. A college professor who gives a lecture to a scholarly organization uses educated formal language; and when he tells friends about his vacation, he uses educated informal language. In his lecture, he will use technical and literary words that he may not normally use when talking about his vacation. This high-level educated language—doctors talking to each other about medicine, lawyers talking to each other about a legal case, computer scientists talking to each other about high-technology developments—includes many technical words that give accuracy to language and serve as abbreviations in rapid communication between specialists, but these words are usually unintelligible to those who are outside the specialty.

There is also uneducated language, the language of people who have limited formal education. This language might be street language in a big city or mountain language in a rural hill community. The people who use uneducated language are not ignorant, indeed they may be quite brilliant, but their language is not the product of formal education. It is the product of the living environment. This language, too, has many special words that make the speech colorful, but also make it unintelligible to those who are outsiders.

Level for Business Correspondence

Most of your business correspondence should be in the common area (that is, shared by both educated and uneducated users) of the language. This guarantees the greatest degree of communication—it is not so educated or formal that most people fail to understand it, nor is it so slangy and informal that people feel it is unimportant or reject it as inappropriate. If you write about a technical subject in your business letter, you will probably use special words that "insiders" know, but these words are generally not in the common area of the language. In this kind of letter, parts of the letter will be in the technical business-correspondence level of the language.

USERS OF ENGLISH AS A SECOND LANGUAGE

If your overseas correspondent learned English as a second language, his English may tend to be schoolbookish, since it is a language he learned at school. He will tend to apply strict dictionary meanings to words and will most often use the primary or major dic-

---

TIP

We use our language at different levels of formality. A person who is speaking to the annual meeting of a company's stockholders uses a different level of vocabulary and grammar than when telling a joke at a backyard barbecue. A person who is interviewing for a job uses a different level of formal language than when describing the interview to a close friend.

tionary definition. He will also tend to use grammar in a precise, but not always accurate or idiomatic, way. In fact, sometimes you may even have the feeling that a schoolchild is writing. Don't be misled by this, however; this correspondent may be brilliant in his field and gifted in his own language but have limited knowledge of English vocabulary and grammar. He needs to be understood at the level of his professional and business competence, and not underestimated because his English usage is somewhat limited.

His "window" on the range of English is smaller than that of a native English user. It is the kind of English taught in high school and university. He also knows specialized English, the kind used in his professional and business life. Since English is such a widely used international language for science and business, his proficiency in this specialized area is probably greater than his proficiency in general usage. Of course, the more exposure he has to English the larger his "window" will become.

From Romance-Language Areas

If your correspondent is from an area where a Romance-language (Spanish, French, Italian, or Portuguese—languages that grew out of Latin) is used, it is necessary to stay alert to possible misunderstandings that can arise because many English words also are based on Latin roots. But even though they share the same Latin original, the words developed differently in English than in Spanish or French. For instance, your Spanish correspondent when writing in English may speak of the "rentability" of a new product. A native English user will first think of the suitability of leasing the product or renting it out. However, your correspondent bases "rentability" on the root *renta*, which means "income in general" or "profit," so the meaning he has in mind when he uses "rentability" is expressed in English by "profitability." (Incidentally, the English word "rent" came from an Old French word *rente*, which meant "income from property"—a meaning that has remained pretty much unchanged in English; whereas in French, the word *rente* has expanded to include the concepts of "income," "dividends," and "interest," as well as "profit.")

Sometimes words have such different ranges of meaning that they can be misleading. In Spanish, the word *profesor* refers to any teacher—whether a kindergarten teacher or the holder of an elite university post. In English, the word "professor" is used only for university or college teachers, except when it is used colloquially to refer to a person of some unusual skill. You may get quite the wrong meaning from your correspondent's letter if you automatically assume he uses the word in the English sense.

TIP

If your overseas correspondent learned English as a second language, his English may tend to be schoolbookish. Don't be misled by this; he may be brilliant in his field and gifted in his own language but have limited knowledge of English vocabulary and grammar. He needs to be understood at the level of his professional and business competence, and not underestimated because his English usage is somewhat limited.

An example often encountered is the use of the word "rationalize." In American English this usually means to "explain away" or to "justify to oneself." But a Spanish-language user (or even a British-English user) bases his use of the word on the root meaning "rational" in the sense of to "think about," so he means to "make organized and logical sense of something and put matters into a logical and coherent framework." When he wants to "rationalize" an organization, he wants to restructure it according to a logical analysis. You can readily see how an American and his overseas correspondent can get quite confused by getting quite different meanings from the same word.

Technical Words

Highly technical words, however, are generally clear to both parties, since they share a common international scientific and professional vocabulary. Accountants mean the same thing by a "credit" or a "debit"; and physiologists mean the same thing by "enzymes" or "hormones."

Your awareness of these characteristics of cross-cultural communication will help you grasp the content of overseas correspondence more accurately. It may also help you to alert your boss to a possible problem if you see confusion beginning to occur. If you have regular correspondence with people from a certain language area—even though the correspondence takes place in English—you should have a bilingual dictionary at hand. Whenever you see an expression that looks sort of normal but doesn't really make good sense, look up key words in the dictionary. You'll usually find that one of the possible definitions makes good sense, even though the meaning that first comes to mind from the appearance of the word is not really clear.

When sending correspondence to foreigners for whom English is a second language, use the same "window" of moderately formal, dictionary-definition English. Use the first and obvious definition of the word rather than the literary and figurative meanings of the word. Better straightforward clarity than a subtle use of the language that only befuddles your reader. Above all, avoid everyday American slang or colloquial language. A Pakistani correspondent, for instance, knows the meaning of "hot" and of "dog." But unless he lived in America, he probably doesn't know what a "hot dog" (something to eat) is. And he almost surely doesn't know the meaning of "Hot dog!" (an expression of great joy or enthusiasm), nor does he describe a person with a showy style of skateboarding or skiing as "a hot dog."

BRITISH ENGLISH

If your correspondent is a native British-English user—whether from England, Nigeria, India, Singapore, or New Zealand—cross-cultural communication is generally easier, but it still is not to be taken for granted. In formal dictionary definitions of many everyday words, there can be confusing differences. British "corn" is American "wheat"; American "corn" is British "maize." British "tin" is American "can" (of vegetables); American "thread" is British "cotton" (for sewing). British "bonnet" is American "hood" (of automobile [British "motor car"]); American "trunk" is British "boot" (in the same automobile); but American "trunk" is also British "portmanteau" (a large, hinged container for packing clothes when traveling).

When slang or informal idiom is used, the differences of meaning between American and British English increase considerably. This is one reason why Americans seldom laugh at British jokes (and the other way around); jokes are usually a play on words at the informal level. When the meaning of the words has to be explained, the suddenness of the unexpected insight (the cause of the humorous reaction) is lost. A joke that has to be explained is no longer funny.

George Bernard Shaw once quipped that Americans and the English were separated by the same language. This witticism contains enough truth to give warning that business correspondence between American and British English users conveys the greatest degree of mutual comprehension when it is conducted in a kind of "mid-Atlantic" English. This is a standard, direct, unidiomatic language that avoids regional color or the latest fad in words.

A SAMPLE LETTER

Here is an annotated sample of a business letter to an overseas correspondent:

February 15, 1995

Sr. Pedro Carcamo-Gonzales
ABC International, S.A.
Apto. 456
123 Avenida del Cinco de Mayo
San Jose, Costa Rica

Dear Sr. Carcamo:

I received your letter of January 3, 1995. In your letter you ask about purchasing software for use in your accounting department.

Our company has an excellent software program for accounting, inventory control, and payroll. Although we developed this software for use on the Zenox Business Microcomputer, we also have versions for use on other popular microcomputers. In your letter, you did not tell us which microcomputer you use. Please tell me the name of the manufacturer, the model number, and the memory capacity (number of bytes) of your microcomputer, and I will send you complete information about the proper software program for your needs.

I look forward to hearing from you soon.

With every good wish, I remain

Yours sincerely,

John P. Wizard
International Services

The following characteristics should be noted:

Date: Most overseas correspondents use a day/month/year sequence when using only figures. Thus, 12/2/95 is February 12, 1995, not December 2, 1995, for most overseas people. Avoid possible confusion by spelling out the month.

Complimentary title: Although you can use "Mr." in addressing overseas correspondents, it is more courteous to use the title appropriate in their own language. In this case, "Sr." stands for *Senor.* You could use *Herr* (German), "M." (French for *Monsieur*), and so on.

Name: Use the proper form of the person's name. In a Spanish-language man's name, the man's mother's family name is part of his formal name. His father's family name is first, and his mother's family name is joined to it by a hyphen. However, when he is addressed directly, only the father's family name is used. Legally and formally he is "Carcamo (father's family name)-Gonzales (mother's family name)," but when spoken to directly he is "Senor Carcamo." A married woman's formal and legal name is made up by joining her father's family name and her husband's family name with "y" ("and"), but she is addressed by her husband's name. Thus, "Sra. Teresa Lopez y Carcamo" would be addressed directly as "Sra. Carcamo." Other languages have other conventions.

By using them correctly, you show that you care about the person and the traditions of his culture. He may be sensitive to note that you have been polite and correct, if you use his name properly; but he will be sure to notice when you use his name improperly. At best he will laugh at your ignorance, and at worst he may take offense at your carelessness.

Box number: In some languages the word for "Post Office Box" may remind you of some other meaning in English. In Spanish the word is *Apartado* or *Apto.* It is not an "apartment." Because the post office personnel in the correspondent's country may not readily understand English, use an address form taken from your correspondent's letterhead to make sure your letter arrives without unnecessary delay.

Body of the letter: Express yourself in clear, direct form. Avoid passives, perfects, and pluperfects as much as possible. Use the present tense, simple past tense, and simple future tense, but avoid conditional future-tense forms whenever possible. Think of your correspondent as an intelligent person who has limited English. Brand names and technical language, however, do not pose any great problem.

Closing: Overseas correspondents tend to be a bit more flowery than American business-letter writers. Therefore, the extra expression of good wishes and personal reference is appropriate.

TIP

Overseas correspondents tend to be a bit more flowery than American business-letter writers. Therefore, the extra expression of good wishes and personal reference is appropriate.

PART III

INSIDE
THE COMPANY

Another entire set of your secretarial relationships is with people and tasks within the company. Primary, of course, is your relationship with your boss and the work you do to make his job easier and more effective. One of your most significant contributions can be that of a buffer, to absorb the little tasks and interruptions that can keep him from performing at his best.

You will also relate to other people in the company on behalf of your boss. How you do it can help or hinder your boss's future in the company.

And much of your time will be spent in performing standard secretarial tasks.

Part III focuses on these relationships and tasks within the company.

CHAPTER 8
DICTATION

Shorthand is a status skill. It provides status for the secretary, since most clerk-typists do not know how to use shorthand. And it provides status for the boss, since she can occasionally dictate to and interact with another person. It makes her feel good. It may even be useful when short memos or instructions are conveyed.

However, in today's electronic office, person-to-person dictating is getting to be very rare. The dictator may use an office dictating machine that rests on her desk or bookcase. Or she may use a portable dictating machine that she can take on trips with her or to her home for overnight or weekend dictating. Or she may use a centralized telephone system, either from her office phone or from any phone anywhere.

POOL DICTATION

The person who transcribes this electronic dictation may be the boss's secretary. In larger offices, it may be a pool typist or an operator in the word-processing department.

If the transcribing is done by someone other than you, you will have to check the work to make sure it is done properly before you turn it over to your boss to sign.

BEGINNING WORRIES

When you first start working with dictation at a new company or with a new boss, your main concern will be to handle the new words that seem to come at you from all sides. Many of these words you've never heard before, and you wonder whether you'll be able to measure up to the constant demand to learn them all.

Be concerned, but don't worry. There are two classes of new words that you will encounter. One group is the technical vocabulary of the company and the business the company is in. The second is the personal vocabulary of your boss. At first you may feel overwhelmed by the number of new words you encounter. But within a very few weeks you will feel at home with them.

Keep in mind that the company's technical vocabulary is limited. The same words keep appearing over and over again as product lines and processes are discussed. As you become familiar with these words in your transcribing, you will soon master the great majority of them. Only now and then will you meet a new group of technical words when some new product or process is developed.

Furthermore, an individual's working vocabulary is also limited. At first it may seem as though your boss knows an exceptionally wide range of words. But as you handle her dictation over hundreds of letters and memos, you will learn that she tends to use the same formulas over and over again. Once you are familiar with the patterns of her dictation, you will have little trouble with unknown words catching you off guard.

After a time you will be so familiar with both the company's and your boss's vocabularies that you will be able to write a letter on a routine subject in your boss's style with very little difficulty. Indeed after you have done this a few times, your boss may routinely tell you to write a letter, giving you only the gist of what she wants included and asking you to put the letter together.

Your Own Word List

As part of your getting to know the special vocabularies of the company and your boss, be sure in the beginning to look up any unfamiliar words in a dictionary to make sure you have the spelling right. You may even want to keep your own speller-divider list in a handy drawer, adding to it as you meet new, repeated words. Having such a list close by will save the time and effort of looking words up each time you encounter them until you have mastered them.

If you use a word processor that has a dictionary or spell-check feature to which you can add words, add these words. Then whenever you spell-check a letter with the word processor, the new words will automatically be included in the checking.

FIRST COPY AS FINAL COPY

For regular letters and memos, prepare your first copy as your final copy for your boss's signature. These letters are expensive enough as it is (considering your boss's time, your time, and machine costs, as well as the cost of postage, paper, and ribbon), so a draft copy for a routine letter is an unneeded luxury.

FIRST COPY AS DRAFT COPY

For longer, highly complex letters or memos and for reports, a draft copy (double-spaced for editing convenience) is probably best. She can usually spot changes she wants to make when she sees the copy in print that she did not sense when she was dictating.

DICTATING REFERENCE NEEDS

Make dictation easier for your boss by putting all the needed resource or reference material together with the letter or memo she is answering. This includes the file of any previous correspondence to the person, as well as any reports or studies referred to by the correspondent in the letter. Any additional names and addresses that will come into consideration in the answer should also be given to your boss with the file.

FINAL FORM

Have your boss clearly indicate at the beginning what form the dictation should take: a letter, a memo, a report. She should indicate whether any special type of stationery is to be used: letterhead (and type of letterhead if she uses more than one), interoffice memo, plain.

She should also indicate the number of copies that will be needed. (This is more important to know at the very beginning if carbon paper is to be used; it is less important to know at the start if you are making photocopies.)

RETENTION OF ORIGINAL

If you are using a word processor, she should also indicate how long she wants the original retained on a diskette or in the central memory unit. She would normally only want to retain a copy in electronic form if she plans to revise the letter sometime in the near future.

PUNCTUATION

Work out a system with her about punctuation. She can dictate each punctuation mark. If she does dictate punctuation marks, you have to be careful not to type out the name of the punctuation as you move along. It can be aggravating to type out the word "period" when the rest of your copy is completely clean. It is probably best for her to indicate any special punctuation she wants, ends of sentences, and ends of paragraphs. Other than that she may want you to punctuate the rest of the letter as needed. Use one of the usage manuals listed in the appendix for simple rules on present-day punctuation. Generally speaking, there are fewer commas used now than were used twenty-five years ago. If your boss is older, she may feel more comfortable with more commas. Either way is correct; it's a matter of personal preference and overall style. Before long you will have a good sense of how your boss likes her dictation punctuated.

ENCLOSURES

Have your boss specify, as part of her dictation, any enclosures she wants sent with the letter. Your problem will be to make sure the enclosures actually go out with the letter. It is so easy to have the letter signed along with several others, slip it in an envelope, and mail it without the enclosures. The best way to ensure that the enclosures are not forgotten is to gather them and give them to your boss as a complete package with the correspondence to be signed and the envelope. Your boss will leaf through them too, which will serve as a double check that all the enclosures have been gathered.

If the complete package is too bulky, then send in a different-colored sheet of paper (yellow, for instance) that lists each enclosure you have collected. The different color reminds you to put the correspondence and the enclosures together when the signed correspondence is sent out for you to mail.

TIP

An individual's working vocabulary is limited. At first it may seem as though your boss knows an exceptionally wide range of words. But as you handle her dictation over hundreds of letters and memos, you will learn that she tends to use the same formulas over and over again.

DISTRIBUTION OF COPIES

Also have your boss specify copy distribution at the time of dictation. If there are outside addressees, she may have to include the name and address. Company addressees will receive their copies by interoffice mail. If your boss sends someone copies of several different letters, it is wise to keep an envelope open for that person throughout the day. Keep adding the copies as they become available, and send the envelope at the close of the day. This is especially important with copies for outside parties because you will want to keep mail costs as low as possible.

SPARE BATTERIES

If your boss uses a portable dictating unit that operates off batteries, keep an extra supply of batteries on hand so you can replace them when they run low. She might not be aware that the batteries are giving out. You will be aware first because the unit will run slower, sometimes unevenly, and her voice will sound lower and increasingly distorted.

SOUNDALIKE WORDS

There are many words in English that sound alike but are spelled differently. These sound-alikes have very different meanings. If your boss is alert to the problem they might cause, she will spell out which one she wants. But more often than not, she does not think of the other word in the midst of her dictating. You can generally figure out which one is the right one by the context in which it appears. Occasionally you might have to ask her which one she wants.

Here are some soundalikes that can easily appear in business correspondence:

accede / exceed

accept / except

addition / edition

access / excess

affect / effect

assistants / assistance

brake / break

coarse / course

cite / sight / site

complement / compliment

correspondents / correspondence

council / counsel / consul

incidents / incidence

its / it's

legislator / legislature

loose / lose

passed / past

personal / personnel

principle / principal

respectfully / respectively

right / write

stationary / stationery

their / there / they're

whose / who's

your / you're

You will develop your own list of soundalikes that occur in your boss's dictation and in the company's vocabulary. Keep in mind that it's (its? it's?) the little ones that cause the most trouble in you're (your is the correct choice here) typing—see what I mean?

CORRECTION MARKS

Work out a standard form for indicating corrections with your boss, so you both know what she wants done when she sends back a letter for revision. It isn't necessary for you both to learn all the standard proofreader's marks, but some simple marks used by them are helpful. (The full set of marks can be found in most college and office dictionaries).

The kinds of corrections normally called for in business correspondence can easily and accurately be noted with the following standard marks:

to entirely change your	Transpose words or letters
send your order	Insert word(s)
⌐	Move to left
	Move to right
9th or NJ	Center on page
	Spell out (ninth or New Jersey)
the President of I.B.M.	Put in lower case (small letters)--president
the president will then	Put in upper case (caps) --President
However the company will	Insert comma (or semicolon)
The answer is yes	Insert period (or colon)
book keeper	Close up
The answer is yes	Add space
call you tomorrow.	Start new paragraph here
Then we can decide	Run in; no paragraph
to entirely change	Delete; remove word(s) or letters

CHAPTER 9

YOUR BOSS'S CALENDAR

Your boss has several important assets: his professional knowledge, his colleagues in the company and in his field, and his time. Your work in correspondence and file maintenance will help him bring his professional knowledge to bear on his job; your reception and telephone work will help advance his relationships with his company and professional colleagues. And your monitoring of his calendar can help him to use his time in the best possible way.

THE IMPORTANCE OF TIME

The importance of an executive's time cannot be stressed enough. Every activity he engages in is at the cost of something else he could have been doing. If your careful monitoring of his calendar can enable him to do fifteen things during the day instead of twelve (or to do those twelve things better because he had a less hassled approach to them by having more time to consider them), you have helped both him and the company considerably.

WHO KEEPS THE MASTER CALENDAR

The first matter you and your boss need to agree on is who keeps the master calendar. Normally you will have a daily calendar on your desk; he will have a pocket calendar he carries with him. (Or he may have a large executive desk calendar that shows a week on a two-page spread and also carry a pocket calendar.) One of these calendars should be designated as the master calendar. Entries into the other calendars should be considered as tentative until they are posted on the master calendar and any conflicts are resolved.

He may wish to keep the master calendar, asking you to present various requests that come in by telephone or correspondence for him to decide upon and enter on his calendar. Or he may ask you to keep it up-to-date, reserving the right to change it from time to time

---

TIP

Your boss has several important assets: professional knowledge, colleagues in the company and in his field, and time.

---

as he sees fit, and then asking you to rearrange appointments that have to be changed.

He will certainly want to retain the right to make any appointment he wishes or to change them as he deems best. However, he may also give you the responsibility of making appoint-

ments for him. If he does, it is all the more important to update all calendars regularly. This avoids the embarrassment of double booking and enables him to cancel any appointment you have made for him that he does not want to keep at that time.

THE DAY IN FIFTEEN-MINUTE SEGMENTS

It is useful to think of his day as consisting in general of fifteen-minute segments (naturally, such a time division is only a guide; very seldom will your boss actually operate on such a tight, regimented schedule). Most people in the company can transact their business in one or two such fifteen-minute segments, usually

one. There is no need for a leisurely get-acquainted period, as there is with a new outside visitor. Nor is there usually the need for a company visitor to brief your boss in detail about the problem; it is often one well known to both and this visit is just a continuing consultation on a continuing matter.

IN-COMPANY VISITORS

You may well ask the person in the company who wants to see your boss how long he expects to take. By asking that, you alert him to the need to keep the visit brief and remind him that your boss has other commitments that make demands upon his time. (Of course, you ask this only of people equal to or lower than your boss in company rank; your boss's boss has the privilege of immediate and untimed access.)

Your regular in-company visitor may say, "I just want to see him for two minutes." Generally, you can count on five, and often it will run on to fifteen. If your boss is really pressed for time, stress that to the visitor. Your boss may be too polite to end the visit as soon as he should to keep the rest of the day in control, especially if the visitor is in the midst of telling the latest joke making the office rounds after having finished his business.

OUTSIDE VISITORS

A visitor from the outside may require two to four fifteen-minute segments. Unless the visit is connected to a lunch date, most business

can be conducted in an hour. If a lunch arrangement is involved, schedule the business visit for the hour before lunch whenever pos-

---

TIP

The importance of an executive's time cannot be stressed enough. Every activity engaged in is at the cost of something else that could have been done.

---

sible. If there are any remaining matters, they are usually discussed during lunch without the person having to return to the office after lunch. If, however, that hour is already scheduled, your boss can meet the person at the restaurant or in your reception room or in his office a few minutes before leaving for lunch. Business will usually be the main agenda at lunch, and any unfinished matters can be dealt with back at the office after lunch. Because

such a luncheon meeting may tend to last somewhat longer than when the same amount of business is conducted in an office setting, you should keep a little leeway on the calendar for the time after lunch. You should remind your boss, however, if he has an appointment soon after the normal lunch hour. That will give him a reason for closing the lunchtime discussion in time to make his next appointment.

TENTATIVE APPOINTMENTS

People often say that they will "pencil" in an appointment, meaning that they are setting it tentatively for now and it will be confirmed at a later time. The idea is that a penciled entry on a calendar can be readily erased if there is a conflict. This may be a useful practice for you

to adopt. Tentative appointments and appointments to be cleared with your boss or others are entered in pencil; firm appointments are entered in ink. By adopting this method, you can tell at a glance which appointments are still awaiting confirmation or clearance.

WHEN YOUR BOSS IS RUNNING LATE

If you see that your boss is running late—either with in-house appointments or with meetings or lunch dates outside the office—and that appointments that are already scheduled are going to be jammed or will have to be postponed, find out from your boss, if possible, which ones he wants put off until later. Call those people and give them a new time, or indicate that your boss sends his apologies for canceling the appointment now and will get back to them later about setting up a new one. If your boss is not available at the time you see schedule trouble brewing, call the

people immediately affected and tell them that your boss is running late, and you will get back to them after you have the opportunity of seeing your boss. You might need to reschedule the appointment. This courtesy will be much appreciated by your boss and by the person whose appointment is affected. Your boss won't really have to apologize for keeping the person waiting or for causing the person to make a visit to no avail; and the person will be flattered that your boss thought enough of him to have you call.

WHO SHOULD KNOW
ABOUT YOUR BOSS'S SCHEDULE

Who your boss sees and where they may go for lunch is his business. You should not volunteer this information if someone calls and wants to know where he is. If the lunch date goes on until 3:30 p.m., don't tell the caller that your boss isn't back from lunch yet. Just say that he isn't available at the present and ask for information so your boss can make a callback later. Most callers will wait until well into the early afternoon before calling. They can be irritated when they are told that your boss is still out to lunch; and they don't really want to hear that he only just left for lunch ten minutes ago. Your office schedule is of little interest to them; they just want to talk to your boss.

APPOINTMENT COURTESIES

An out-of-town visitor usually tries to have four or five business appointments during each day he is in town in order to make the trip as worthwhile as possible. This is especially true if he is in town only for the day and has airline schedules and traffic congestion to the airport he must include in his planning. Anything you and your boss can do to accommodate his timing request will be much appreciated by the visitor. He will understand that there are meetings and earlier commitments that cannot be adjusted, but he will also be most grateful for your meeting his requests as closely as possible. And your boss may hope for the same kind of accommodation when he sets up an itinerary for his out-of-town business trips.

It is a courtesy for out-of-town visitors to keep a map of your city and general area in your desk. From time to time a visitor will have to go to another office he has never visited before and which he doesn't know how to reach from your office. You may not know how yourself, but being able to look at local maps for a few minutes might save your visitor valuable time and much anguish.

If he is running a little late, you can offer him the use of a telephone to call his next appointment. This will save him the time and anxiety of looking for a public telephone somewhere in your office building or in some public place outside.

APPOINTMENTS WITH JUNIORS

When your boss asks you to make an appointment with someone who works for him, it is courteous to let the person know the general subject your boss wants to discuss. This allows the person to prepare himself, thus making the meeting more productive for both people. Otherwise, the person may wonder whether he is being called on the carpet or even faces dismissal. The imagination can create all sorts of unpleasant scenarios. And unless your boss has such an unpleasant task to perform, there is little need for a summons to his office to arouse unnecessary free-floating anxiety. The person may have enough to do to get ready to see your boss without carrying the weight of the unknown.

TIP

Who your boss sees and where they may go for lunch is his business. You should not volunteer this information if someone calls and wants to know where he is. If the lunch date goes on until 3:30 p.m., never tell the caller that your boss isn't back from lunch yet.

APPOINTMENTS
WITH PEERS AND SENIORS

Normally your boss will make his own appointments with his equals and his boss. Occasionally he may ask you to call the other person's secretary to see if that person will be in that day or might be free for lunch or at a particular hour. But then your boss would probably use that information when making the appointment.

> **

CHAPTER 10

OFFICE APPEARANCE

The general appearance of your office and your boss's office is an advertisement about how you run your business. A sloppy office suggests to the visitor that he will suffer from sloppy treatment in the long run. A cold, austere atmosphere suggests that the visitor will be treated with little human warmth or understanding. A neat, but obviously active, workplace that has touches of personal interest suggests that the visitor will be treated personally and efficiently by a busy but in-control company.

The amount of personal decorating that you can introduce into your own work space is dictated by company policy and the office environment. If it is a large office with standardized modules and work spaces that have been carefully coordinated by an office designer, there will be little opportunity for much personalization of your own space. A personal picture or two, a hanging calendar or poster, some flowers or personal accessories on your desk, these are the most that will normally be allowed—or are acceptable—in a standardized, designed office.

If you are in a smaller, older office, a few more personal effects can be brought in to create your own space. However, your office should not become your "home away from home." Keep your home at home, and make your office a pleasant, cheerful *working* place.

If you are located outside your boss's office, rather than in your own office, you will have fewer choices. And even they should be discussed with her, since they serve as an entry to her own office. Here I am talking more about a dramatic, colorful poster on the wall than I am about a small family picture on your desk or the choice of desk accessories.

Since you have to spend eight hours of each working day in this office, you want it to be as pleasing and relaxing in appearance as possible. But you also have to take into consideration the fact that it is also a place where others also spend eight hours of their working day. The degree to which you can personalize your environment increases as you move from a pool situation, to an office-related wall, to your own office.

Included in your personal effects is your own professional bookshelf. This should include books about secretarial usage and practice that you have purchased, wordbooks and dictionaries, stylebooks and professional or trade books about your company's business. Some of these books will be provided by the

---

TIP

Your office should not become your "home away from home." Keep your home at home, and make your office a pleasant, cheerful *working* place.

---

company, some are your own. They should be readily available. They make a pleasing appearance against a stark wall. As they become well used, they give an impression of professionalism to passing visitors.

As you work, you tend to spread papers and files around you. Each time you finish a particular job, put the papers and files away before starting on the next job. This way the clutter never gets out of control. Before lunch and at the end of each day, do a general tidying up. This is the time to pick up stray paper clips, put the adhesive tape back where you usually keep it, put extra pencils back in the drawer or in your pencil holder, cover your typewriter or dust your word processor, and put all your diskettes in their proper place.

You can keep your own work space neat and organized. You will have less control over the appearance of your boss's office. Much depends on whether she is a "clean desk" type or a "cluttered desk" type. Your job will be greatly simplified if she leans toward the clean-desk habit. She will then regularly give you files of papers to sort through and handle.

If, however, she tends to be more cluttered, you will have to work out with her a mutually agreeable pattern on handling her papers: Does she, for example, want you to go through the papers on her desk every day or so to remove those no longer needed and to put those in order that she is working on? You may even have to remind her, now and then, about the relative urgency of a paper you discovered lying at the bottom of a pile that

should have been acted on earlier. The clutter type of boss tends, now and then, to lose track of a piece of paper. Part of your job is to know what is still pending that is on her desk so when questions come up about it, you know where it is and can bring it to your boss's attention.

With the clutter type, keep moving as many papers as you can from her desk into the files. You can always get them again if they are needed. The clutter type will tend to hold on to papers for longer than she needs them rather than send them out for filing when she should. Your discreet management of her desk top will not only keep her office looking neater, but it will also provide better long-term management of her paperwork.

In keeping both your office and your boss's office generally neat, you should not take on maintenance and cleaning jobs. Let the office cleaners do their work. But when there is a noticeable problem that is not likely to resolve itself, you can initiate a solution to the problem. If, for instance, a visitor spills a cup of coffee over a sofa and onto the rug, you should bring the matter to the attention of the maintenance department or the cleaners so it can be thoroughly cleaned before the stains set. If a chair leg breaks, that, too, should be called to the attention of the maintenance department for repair or replacement. Make the system work to provide the right level of maintenance. For this reason, it is good to develop a supportive, rather than a critical, relationship with the head of the maintenance

---

TIP

You can keep your own work space neat and organized. You will have less control over the appearance of your boss's office.

---

department. Much can be accomplished quicker with a show of personal regard than can often be done through formal memos or complaining phone calls.

CHAPTER 11
DRESS FOR SUCCESS

There are several books available on dressing for success in the business world. Most of them are written for people who have had little exposure to the business environment and who want their clothes to make a statement about their professional capability. They are also written for people who have little confidence in their own clothes sense and who seek guidance from people who have far more experience in the business world than they do.

However much you may feel confident in your own clothes decisions and however much you may have set your own style, a brief glance through one of these books can be enlightening and helpful.

You can make the mistake of dressing below the level of responsibility you have. If you have been promoted from a clerk-typist position, or from a typing or word-processing pool, you have probably dressed to fit in with your peers. Now you've moved up in the company and that style of dress may no longer be advisable in your new position. You also have to consider the rank your boss holds in the company and dress in a way that he, his visitors, and his peers might think appropriate. You may have to switch from faded denims to flannel slacks, or from pants to skirts,

or from casual sportswear to suits or blazers, or from athletic shoes to street shoes.

There is no clear, standardized formula for appropriate dress. The once-critical rules have given way in recent years to a great deal of flexibility. Much also depends on the region of the country in which you work. For instance, I now work and live near the ocean where the "uniform of the day" includes boating shoes. I wear them to work; my dentist wears them at his office; my lawyer wears them at his; and my accountant wears them when he calls on me, as does my banker when I visit him. However, when I visit clients in New York or Boston, I do not wear boating shoes. Nor do people who work in a nonboating region—say, in Denver—wear boating shoes as part of their working dress.

The dress-for-success suggestions are generally directed to people who want to succeed in the major cities of the country. Adapt their suggestions to the conditions in the region where you work.

If it is important not to underdress for your position in the company, it is also important not to overdress. The degree of formality in dress appropriate for the secretary of the corporate president may be too overpowering if

---

TIP

It is important not to underdress for your position in the company; it is also important not to overdress.

---

worn by the secretary of a junior officer. Unwritten dress standards are set by the practice in the region, in the city, and in your own company. Using your own eyes and your sense of good judgment, determine what feels right for your present position, and at the same time helps you appear to be a reasonable candidate for a higher position. Although your work will create a reputation for you in the company, your appearance will also have an impact on executives in the firm. An appearance of disciplined, personable efficiency as shown by your dress makes an immediate impression that will cause them to look more carefully at your work performance. An inappropriate pattern of dress will unfairly create an impression that will cause them to take your work less seriously than they would if you dressed appropriately.

If you have a limited budget for clothes, I suggest you go for classics—clothes that don't come and go with each passing season. Keep those fashions for your afterwork activities. Buy for quality. I personally prefer natural fibers to synthetic fibers, feeling that they are more comfortable, easier to keep clean,

and that their quality is readily seen. Buy neutral colors: the blacks, tans, blues, and grays. Add other colors in the accessories: blouses, shirts, ties, scarves, sweaters, and so on. A classic blazer, slacks/skirt combination can last for several seasons, with continual change achieved by changing accessories.

Quality clothes will hold up well for several seasons, both in condition and in fashion. Inexpensive clothes will fall apart quickly, will not hold their shape, will seldom fit right in the first place, and will become dated quickly. Over the long run, it is really cheaper to buy fewer but better clothes for work than to buy more but less expensive clothes. It is surprising how little more it takes to buy quality clothes. This is especially true if you study the features of good clothing (stitching, lining, styling, material—see a book from the library on clothing characteristics) and then look for such clothing in reputable discount stores. Perhaps as much as 90 percent of clothing in many such stores is not up to the quality you would desire, but if you find that 10 percent and recognize it, you can stretch your clothing dollar. One discount house advertises with the

---

TIP

Unwritten dress standards are set by the practice in the region, in the city, and in your own company. Using your own eyes and your sense of good judgment, determine what feels right for your present position, and at the same time helps you appear to be a reasonable candidate for a higher position.

---

slogan, "An educated consumer is our best customer." Educate yourself about quality in clothing, and you will dress better for less.

How you dress for the office also affects how you feel about yourself and your work. If you don't take your job seriously and if you have a low opinion of yourself, your dress will somehow reflect those feelings. If, however, you feel good about yourself and you feel your job is important to you, your dress will also show those feelings. In fact, there is such a close interconnection between your feelings and your dress that you can help enhance good feelings about yourself and your job by dressing as if you already had those feelings. Then, when you glance at yourself in a window as you pass by, or you sense someone looking at you with appreciation, or you know how right you look, you will usually seem inwardly to grow into your expectations. Dress is as much for your morale and sense of self-esteem as it is for your job setting.

CHAPTER 12

GUARDING THE DOOR

As the keeper of the gate, you are the person through whom most people in the company make arrangements to see your boss. Constant decisions have to be made about who to let in, who to postpone, who to help, who to discourage. The conflict is between your boss's need to know what the person has to say or the importance of her answer to the person's questions and the protection of her time and privacy so she can do things she needs to do.

The person who comes may really need your boss's answers, or he may come primarily to call attention to himself on the pretext of asking your boss a business question.

Some bosses have an open-door policy. They keep the door to their office open, and everyone who wants to see her can just walk in. This kind of boss probably remembers the frustrations she felt trying to see her boss, and she determined that people who worked with her would always have access. Generally, this works well, except this kind of boss is very much at the mercy of the people who want to see her for frivolous as well as serious matters. Time for concentration on working out her own tasks is always interrupted, thus adversely affecting the quality of her own output.

Some bosses go to the opposite extreme. Their door is always closed; people can see them only by appointment or summons. They control who they see and when, and you are the receptionist. Somewhere in between is the boss who works behind a closed door when she wants to concentrate or to see someone privately, and who opens her door as a sign that people are free to drop by briefly to see her. This kind of boss is more likely to use you as a guardian of the door.

She may want you to interrupt her when the door is closed but someone comes with a genuine emergency. She may want you to put

---

TIP

When turning a visitor away, you do not want to give the impression that his problem is insignificant or that he does not count.

through a telephone call even though she has a visitor if that call is one she has been trying to complete for some time. But she may also want you to turn away anyone who would interrupt her while she is preparing a report, assuring them that she will get in touch with them later in the afternoon. And she may want you to hold all calls while she has a visitor, telling the caller that she will call back the next morning. This kind of boss will learn to let you make the judgment about the urgency of an interruption as you both get to know each other.

One of the sensitive problems in guarding the door is the matter of perspective. Your boss—and, hence, you—have a much wider view of the company and its priorities than does someone who works in a specialized area under your boss. What that person sees as vital probably is so in the performance of his work or in the level of responsibility he has in the company. But from the perspective your boss has that person's problem is much less urgent than some other problem at present to be dealt with. When turning the visitor away, you do not want to give the impression that his problem is insignificant or that he does not count, even though you know your boss has more important matters before her at the

moment. You must reassure the visitor that your boss will soon get back to him. In fact, your boss may later give you the answer to convey to this person; you must tell him it's from your boss so he continues to feel that he was heard at the boss's level. In fact, it is important to bring the concerns of each visitor you turned away or postponed to your boss's attention as soon as you can. Many major problems started as minor ones that were ignored until it was too late.

Some bosses like a diary to be kept of who they see and for how long. For certain professionals, such as lawyers, this information is important for billing purposes. For other executives it is important for record purposes. This is particularly true in the case of government officials. If these records are needed or desired by your boss, she may ask you to note in a diary who comes to see her and the times of their arrival and departure. This diary is different from an appointment book. The appointment book does not necessarily contain everyone who slips in and out, nor are all appointments kept as scheduled. The appointment book is the plan of the day; the diary is the record of the actual day itself. Such a diary, if routinely maintained, is acceptable as a legal record of fact.

CHAPTER 13

ROUTINES
AND REMINDER SYSTEMS

A critical factor in business success is getting things done on time. To do so requires planning, scheduling, and schedule monitoring.

These are included in the services a secretary can perform, provided your boss wants you to and provided you work together on it.

ROUTINES

Some business tasks are routine. I use the word "routine" in the sense of regularly scheduled tasks, which are to be performed at stated times each day, each week, each month, or each quarter. You and your boss should discuss thoroughly what routine tasks he has to perform, and what routine tasks he wants you to perform. You should list these on the master calendar.

If the task is a rather simple one, you need list it only on the day it is to be done. However, if the task requires considerable preparation, you should list the preparation day as well as the day of the task on the master calendar. For instance, if your boss has a monthly heads-of-departments meeting to attend, you should list the day of the meeting on the calendar. But if it takes him two or three days to prepare for the meeting, you should list "Prep: Dept. Heads Mtg." sufficiently ahead of the day of the meeting so that he will have adequate preparation time. Just which day or

days are preparation time depends on the rest of his schedule during that period.

The reasons for using the master calendar to record the due dates for routine tasks are:

1. To avoid having to record dates in different locations.

2. To avoid having to look up dates in different locations.

3. To be able to see the week's work schedule at a glance so the proper amount of time can be allocated to each task as the week proceeds. This avoids, as much as possible, hassled, half-done work at the last minute to meet a deadline.

4. To be able to see at a glance the impact an unexpected appointment or business trip will have on accomplishing in a timely manner the routine tasks that are due to be performed.

TIP

A critical factor in business success is getting things done on time.
To do so requires planning, scheduling, and schedule monitoring.

Some secretaries enter the routine tasks in a unique color. All routine tasks are, for example, listed in green. This enables you and your boss to tell instantly which entries are appointments and which are tasks to be done. The heads-of-departments meeting would be in blue or black ink, since it is an appointment. The preparation for the meeting would be in green ink, since it is a task that has to be included in the day's activities.

You and your boss have to work out which routine tasks are his alone, which are yours, and which ones require you to collect information or do certain preliminary tasks for him before he can complete the task. As the months go on, you will probably be able to accomplish an increasing number of the routine tasks yourself, freeing your boss for other work.

REMINDER SUGGESTIONS

Many business tasks are not routine in nature, but the deadline for their performance is known some time in advance. For instance, your boss may have told a major customer that he will send advance information about a new line of equipment as soon as engineering makes a report about the performance of the equipment. Engineering is due to make the report at the July heads-of-department meeting. You need to remind your boss to send information to the customer within a day or two after the meeting.

Tickler File

The easiest way to keep track of nonroutine tasks is to keep a "tickler" file. The word comes from the idea of tickling your memory. A tickler file consists of twelve folders—one for each month of the year—and thirty-one folders—one for each day of the month. The system is a little complex to explain, but easy to work:

1. You write a task and the date it is to be done on a piece of paper and place it in the month file. Or you photocopy a piece of correspondence in which the task is discussed, write the date on which it is to be accomplished in large letters, and place the copy in the month file. You add new tasks to the proper month's file whenever you learn of them.

2. You place the thirty-one-folder set behind the current month's divider. Then you sort out that month's tasks by day, putting the proper tickler sheets in the folder for the day on which the task is to be done. You can add new sheets as the month goes on and as new tasks come up. If a task is not done on the day it was tickled for, do not leave the sheet in the folder for that day. It will only be forgotten there until the same date next month. Reassign a new date for the task and place the sheet in the proper folder.

TIP

Do not trust your memory to remember to do something. Write it down.

---

3. Each evening look at the next day's tickler file, and build those items into your boss's schedule or your own, as appropriate. If your boss is taking a trip, you can both go over the tickler file for the days he will be gone to decide how those matters are to be handled.

4. For the year ahead you may want to have a set of folders by quarters. However, when you finish with January this year, put that file at the end of the 12 monthly files and it becomes January of the following year. Do the same with February, and so on through the year. You will need the quarter files only for items scheduled well into the year ahead.

5. If you postpone acting on a tickler sheet until it is no longer proper or reasonable to act

on the task, destroy the sheet rather than continue to clutter up the tickler system with it. This ensures that your tickler system is one you really use, not just a place to keep undone tasks off your desk and out of sight. Your tickler system should consist of notes and photocopies of correspondence only; all originals are kept in the permanent file. Nothing of record is lost when you destroy a tickler sheet.

6. When you do the task, destroy the tickler sheet. It has served its purpose and there is no need to clutter up your files with tickler-sheet photocopies of originals that are already on file. If you have any correspondence that is a part of doing the task, that correspondence will be filed as part of the record.

DAILY REMINDER NOTES

Keep a pad of plain notepaper on your desk for short notes to yourself. I have found 3″ x 5″ paper is a convenient size, since you have enough room for a fairly lengthy note, and it is right for just a telephone number. Letter-sized paper (8½″ x 11″) is wasted when used for short reminder notes.

These notes are things to do during the day, or things to talk to your boss about that day. If the task is to be done at a later time, put it into the tickler system.

Don't trust your memory to remember to do something. Your attention is all too easily and quickly transferred to too many things to trust your ability to remember each little detail of something you thought of doing, said you would do, or were asked to do.

Write one item per sheet of notepaper. Line them up on the side of your desk so you can see them. If they get buried, they will be forgotten. Every time you take an action, throw the note related to that action out.

Often your day will have flurries of hectic, pressure-filled activity; then there will be periods of relative quiet. Take advantage of the quieter times to do some of the tasks on your reminder notes.

Part of your success as a secretary depends on the reputation you acquire in the company. Don't get the reputation of being someone who says she will do something, but never does it or forgets to do it. It won't take long for such a reputation to develop if you make promises you fail to keep or are asked to do

---

TIP

Don't get the reputation of being someone who says she will do something, but never does it or forgets to do it.

---

things you just didn't remember to do. The regular, faithful use of your calendar for reminding you about routine tasks, of a working tickler system for reminding you about nonroutine tasks, and of a desk memo pad for little tasks that come up during the day will ensure the highest possible reputation for dependability. The more that people find out that they can rely on you, the more that reliability will be recognized and rewarded.

CHAPTER 14
MEMOS

Memo writing is a communications form all its own. The dictionary defines a memorandum as a short note whose purpose is to serve as a reminder or a written record or communication. Most people use "memo" when speaking about a memorandum. Although the formal plural is "memoranda," most people in everyday office usage refer to them as "memos." Generally, the only place the word "memorandum" is consistently used is as a heading for a preprinted or typed sheet of paper.

DIRECT STYLE FOR MEMO WRITING

When writing a memo, the normal style is to get right into the subject matter. The letter-writing conventions of a formal address and salutation are not a part of memo-writing style. There are generally no personal comments, which are usually included in a business letter between friends to personalize the business contained in the letter. A memo can sometimes be more informal than a business letter to a stranger; but if it is a memo that serves as a formal aide-mémoire, the language is direct and formal. An aide-mémoire is a recording of events and agreements for the record; its purpose is to recall to memory what happened.

TYPES OF MEMOS

Your boss may use memos for a number of reasons:

1. To remind someone to do something.

2. To explain to her boss (or others) why she did (or did not) do something.

3. To get a matter on the record in writing, an aide-mémoire. This may be a "memo to the file" so that your boss, or whoever handles the file in the future should she be transferred, will have this information available. A "memo to the file" is usually the summary of a telephone conversation or the result of a thought about the situation. Or it may be a matter about which your boss thinks there may be some trouble or conflict in the future. By dictating a memo now, your boss is protecting herself against possible criticism or confrontation sometime in the future. Usually, this type of memo is dictated to someone, with a spread of copies, so that the record is duly registered with a number of others.

4. To "blast" someone in the presence of others. "The presence of others" is provided by those listed as receiving copies. This rather harsh use of a memo may backfire by starting a memo blitz of charges, countercharges, defenses, and positions taken. One of the dangers in using memos in the conduct of intraoffice warfare is the way it forces people to take firm public positions. Any movement away from a position is then seen as a victory for someone and a defeat for someone else.

5. To convey information. This information can be about products, procedures, personnel, strategies, schedules, or any matter of interest to people in the company.

6. To make a proposal or a report. A proposal or report in memo form is not as formal as one in report form. The matter being proposed or reported on may not be of the magnitude appropriate to a full-fledged proposal or report, though the matter still needs to be on paper.

7. To send an indirect message. An indirect message is sent by including the person for whom the message is really intended (but to whom it is not addressed) on the copy list. Your boss might not normally write directly to this person on this subject, but she wants to get a message to him. So she writes the memo to someone she would be expected to write it to, but "sneaks" the message to the person she really wants by listing him as a copy. A second way of sending an indirect message by memo is to copy someone who is a threat to the person to whom the memo is written. It is somewhat like saying, "You'd better pay attention to this because Mr. Montague now knows about it." In a sense, your boss is calling on Mr. Montague's power in the organization to back her up or to intimidate the person to whom the memo is addressed.

FORMS FOR WRITING MEMOS

Memos can be short—a single line—or long—several pages. They can be handwritten on a small desktop memo pad, or they can be typed on a printed memorandum form. Increasingly, they can be written on a small desktop or portable computer and printed out by a dot-matrix printer on a roll of tape paper. The part of the tape with the memo on it is then torn off and is stapled to a regular memo sheet or letterhead sheet. This identifies the originator and ensures that the little piece of paper does not get lost. Or they can be written on a computer and entered into an electronic mail system. Other people in the system log in to see if there are

any memos for them, and they can see the memo on their screen and get a hard-copy printout, if they want one.

Memo Pads

If you have anything to say about the wording of small desktop memo pads, have them say "Memo from Miss Anne Smith" or "Memo from Anne Smith" or just the company logo and "Anne Smith." Please do not have them say "From the Desk of Anne Smith," if you can help it. I have never enjoyed receiving memos from someone's desk.

FILE COPIES

You will have to exercise judgment about keeping copies of memos that your boss originates. If it is a short, personal note confirming a lunch date, there is no reason to keep a copy—at least beyond the date of the lunch. You already have a record of the date on your master calendar. If, however, it discusses a matter of substance, a copy should be kept in the file. It can be very important as part of an extended discussion on the matter, as memos and letters on the subject build up over a course of several weeks, months, or even years.

ELEMENTS IN A MEMO

Date

Normally, a memo follows a standard form. At the top, usually centered, is the word "Memorandum" or "MEMORANDUM." The name of the company may also be printed at the head of the paper, but this is not generally of letterhead quality. The "Date" is placed on a line below the word "Memorandum."

From/To

Then there is a "From/To" section. It makes little practical difference which is first. It is more a matter of house preference. Some organizations like "From" first, so the originator is readily identified. Others like "To" first, believing that gives the memo a more courteous flavor. Personally, I like "From" first: It gets right to business, saying who is writing the memo.

Subject

Then there is a "Subject" section. This provides for a short description of the subject the memo deals with. The subject section is useful to focus attention on the point of the memo, and it serves as a handle for filing purposes.

Body

The body of the memo follows. Many memo writers number their points—more often than they would do so in letter writing—to highlight their outline of thought. When people respond or comment on the memo, they can more easily refer to a statement in "item 4" than they can to "the fifth paragraph on page 2." Numbering points also makes it easier for those who receive copies of the memos to follow the development of comments by making it easy to locate points that are being discussed.

Copies

The final section of the memo contains a list of those who were sent copies of the memo. Usually, this list is alphabetical. In

---

TIP

Memos can be short—a single line; or long—several pages.

some companies, the list is by seniority, or at least the president or chief executive officer is at the head of the list. And in some companies, people who are not in the company but who might be copied for the memo are listed at the head of the list, whereas company recipients are listed alphabetically. Depending on company style, the list is by last name only (Henshaw), by initial and last name (R. Henshaw), by social title and last name (Miss Henshaw), by name and department (Henshaw, Product Planning), or by first and last name (Ruth Henshaw). Your boss will tell you the standard form to use in your company,

even though she gives you only a list of last names.

It is important that the copy list be complete. Apart from those times your boss is using copies for indirect messages, you should review the list in the light of who has received copies of previous memos on the same subject. If someone has been left out, you should call that to your boss's attention. The omission may have been merely an oversight, or it may have been deliberate. Only she knows which. Your job is to make sure oversights do not happen.

YOUR MEMOS

There are times when you will write a memo in your own name. If, for instance, your boss asks you to make sure the rug is cleaned in her office before October 10 because she is having some important visitors on that date. The rug cleaning is long overdue, and this visit provides a good reason for finally getting it done. You would send a memo to the person in charge of maintenance. It would be clear, but personal. Clear because you are carrying

out an order that you want accomplished on time for everyone's sake; personal because you will continue to have to call on maintenance to do things for you and your boss. You may telephone maintenance to discuss the rug cleaning, but you send the memo for confirmation and to get the matter in writing for the record in case there is any problem in getting the job done on time.

SAMPLE MEMOS

Some sample memos follow, using a variety of memo formats.

1. A memo to convey information and rearrange a schedule:

MEMORANDUM

March 15, 1989

From: Karen Smith
To: Al Twining

Subj: Schedule Change for Meeting with Delray Inc.

The meeting with the development engineers at Delray has been postponed until April 18 at 10:30 a.m. The meeting is now scheduled to be held at their office in San Pablo.

The reason for the delay, so Delray tells me, is that they have had some trouble getting their TIRESIAS AI program and their knowledge engineer to sync on the needs of our customer. It seems that the inferences from the data are not making sense to the people at GT.

Let's have breakfast together at 7:30 a.m. on April 18 at Dempsey's on Route 161, review the situation as it is then, get our questions and requirements in order, and drive over together to Delray.

Copies: Bill Andrews
        Martha Belmont
        Ron Montague
        Tom Speare

2. A memo to confirm a request for action and to get the request and agreement to act on the record:

MEMORANDUM

September 3, 1990

From: Jane Dow
To: Rich Turner

Subj: Cleaning Miss Smith's Carpet

This confirms our phone conversation earlier this morning about cleaning Miss Smith's carpet. She has asked that it be cleaned before October 6 so it will be dry by the tenth. You said you've got it scheduled for the night of October 4. Great! I know it'll look 1,000 percent better.

Thanks, Rich, for getting this done in time. Miss Smith asked me to pass along her thanks, too.

Copy: Miss Smith

3. A memo to report the results of a meeting, serving as an aide-mémoire, or getting the matter on the record for the future:

MEMORANDUM

April 19, 1989

From: Karen Smith
To: Ron Montague

Subj: Delray/GT problems

1. Sam Johnson at Delray called on March 14, asking that our meeting with them be postponed until mid-April. He reported that the GT people were not happy with the results they were getting from the prototype results of merging the TIRESIAS Artificial Intelligence program with the input provided by the knowledge engineer (Warren McDowell of Knowledge Systems Inc.).

2. Al Twining and I had a meeting at Delray on April 18 with Sam Johnson and some of his people, together with Dan Robbins of GT. The upshot of the day's discussion is that GT has lost confidence in Knowledge Systems's ability to debrief the experts at GT on spacial guidance systems. GT believes that the TIRESIAS AI inferences are not sound because the expert knowledge base the inferences are constructed on are inaccurate. They do not believe Knowledge Systems has been able to capture the subtleties in the expert knowledge GT's spacial-guidance people possess; and GT is convinced that no one at Knowledge Systems has the capability of getting that expert knowledge stated correctly.

3. The meeting came to the following decisions:
    a. No one wants to lose the data Knowledge Systems has already obtained. Knowledge Systems/GT/Delray/and ourselves will find a knowledge systems expert to complement the work done so far by Knowledge Systems.
    b. GT will undertake the search for this expert. He must meet with their approval.

c. The GT-recruited expert will be contracted by Knowledge Systems. His costs will be absorbed by Knowledge Systems within the parameters of their budget arrangements with Delray.

d. The expert must be on board by November 15. He will have two months to familiarize himself with the project and the current status of the project.

4. This restructuring will result in a possible four-month delay to our latest estimate of end-time completion date. GT can live with this, according to Dan Robbins, provided the new expert does indeed work out.

5. We need to keep a close watch on GT's recruitment effort. Al Twining is preparing a list of possible candidates for Dan Robbins. Dan will have that list on April 20. Al and Dan will jointly interview all possibles, so we will have a good reading on how the process goes.

6. The next full-scale review (Knowledge Systems/GT/Delray/us) will be at 10:30 a.m. on Wednesday, May 15, in our conference room.

Copies: Sam Johnson (Delray)
       Warren McDowell (Knowledge Systems Inc.)
       Dan Robbins (GT)
       Bill Andrews
       Martha Belmont
       Tom Speare
       Al Twining

c. The GT-retained expert will be contracted by Knowledge Systems. His costs will be absorbed by Knowledge Systems within the parameters of their budget arrangements with us.

d. The expert must be on board by November 15. He will have two months to familiarize himself with the project and the current status of the project.

4. This restructuring will result in a possible four-month delay in our latest estimate of end-time completion date. GT can live with this, according to Dan Robbins, provided the new expert does indeed work out.

5. We need to keep a close watch on GT's recruitment effort. Al Twerling is preparing a list of possible candidates for Dan Robbins. Dan will have that list on April 25. Al and Dan will jointly interview all possibles, so we will have a good reading on how the process goes.

6. The next full-site review (Knowledge Systems/GT/DoD review) will be at 10:30 a.m. on Wednesday, May 15, in our conference room.

                    Copies: Sam Johnson (Delrny)
                            Waren McDowell (Knowledge Systems Inc.)
                            Don Robbins (GT)
                            D.J. Andrews
                            Marsha Belmont
                            Tom Spicer
                            Al Twerling

CHAPTER 15

REPORTS

Reports are part of business and government life. Your boss is assigned a task to research. He then has to make recommendations for approval and action. Or he may think of something he wants to initiate or an improvement he sees can be made. Research and a report is the way to bring the matter before others and to get a decision.

People always say, "I want to see it on paper." They want a concise report they can use as the basis for rendering a judgment. They also want the report to serve as a part of the record, so they can refer back to it as the basis for later explaining their decision or for making further decisions.

Report writing is mainly your boss's job. But preparing the report in a form that is clear, readable, and persuasive in appearance is yours. You may not have much to say about what it says, but you can influence how it looks.

Some companies have standard report formats. If that is true of your company, study previous reports or reports presented by other executives (you can usually borrow a copy from another secretary) to find out how the company wants its reports to look.

The elements that make up a standard report follow:

1. Title page

The page is similar to the title page of a book. It gives essential information at a glance: the title of the report; the name of the person or group that wrote the report; the date of the report; and the department or company in which the report originated. Here is a sample title page.

A PROPOSAL FOR

THE ACQUISITION OF

MICROTECH DATA, INC.

Squantum, Massachusetts

October, 1988

Prepared by
John R. Smith

Computronics International

2. Executive summary

Many reports have a one-page summary of the report as the first page of the report. It is called an "executive summary" in that it is prepared for busy executives who want to see at a single, brief reading what the report is all about and where it leads to. Usually, the executive summary is written last, even though it is the first page to follow the title page. When writing it, your boss will usually be able to sense whether certain parts of his development of the main body of the report are weak, and he may decide to do some further writing or editing at that time.

The executive summary should contain the following sections: (1) purpose of the report; (2) main points discussed, listed numerically in outline form; and (3) action recommendations, listed numerically and in order of importance. The executive summary should never be more than a single page. It therefore may be necessary to type it single-spaced. Here is a sample executive summary.

A Proposal for the Acquisition of
MICROTECH DATA, INC.

Executive Summary

1. Purpose.

This proposal reports the results of a study concerning the possible acquisition of MICROTECH DATA, INC. by Computronics International to provide us with a software-product company that will augment our equipment line.

2. Our need for a software line.

In order to supply our customers with adequate software for our computer equipment, we need either to license or acquire an experienced software-product company, one that has a full complement of programmers already in place and that has a proven track record of creating successful product. To develop our own internal software-product division would be too costly and too time-consuming. It is a field we do not have direct experience in and we would lose valuable market time in learning about the field and in attracting the right personnel.

3. Licensing is unsatisfactory.

If we enter into a licensing agreement with a software firm, we are only one of several companies served. Our needs are such that we cannot afford to be just one of several; we need full-time attention to software development for our equipment and for major marketing efforts.

4. Microtech Data, Inc.

Microtech Data, Inc., is the right company for us to acquire at this time. Its history, personnel on hand, marketing know-how, and present financial condition are a good blend for acquisition right now.

5. Recommendation.

That we proceed to negotiate acquisition of Microtech Data, Inc., with a view to completed takeover no later than December 12, 1988.

As a result of reading the executive summary, an executive who receives a copy of the report may react in any one of a number of ways:

a. He may decide the report contains information only for him. The executive summary gives him enough information for his purposes, and he has the report filed in case he is ever called on to refer to it again.

b. The executive decides he is concerned about the subject discussed in the report, so he reads the entire report in great detail to fill himself in on all the supporting material that backs up the executive summary. He may send for more information to obtain further support or he may challenge some information or the conclusions your boss has drawn from the data.

c. The executive has to make a decision based on the material in the report. He not only reads it in detail, but he calls your boss in for further consultation about various points your boss has made and recommendations for action he has presented. He assigns some further research on one or two points to your boss before he (the senior executive) presents the matter to a committee. The executive summary, however, is the skeleton around which he structures his presentation and recommendations.

3. The main body of the report

The report is usually divided into sections, based on an overall outline. These sections can include: background (introductory material that puts the report into perspective); purpose (what the report is designed to achieve); definition of terms (if words are used in a technical sense in the report, a glossary of these terms early in the report will help ensure that the reader understands the words to mean the same thing that the writer does); points in the outline (main sections that describe research done, facts uncovered, areas investigated, and the like); and recommended or required actions (depending on whether the report is going up the chain of authority for consideration or down the chain for implementation).

It is important in a report to have enough divisions of the material at logical places of division and to have them labeled. This gives the reader guideposts throughout the report so he can know what he is looking at, where he has been, and where he is going. These guideposts are called "heads." Normally, a report will have two levels of heads (A and B heads); it might have as many as four (A, B, C, and D heads). To help the reader know which is which and how they relate to each other, it is useful for each type of head to look differently typographically.

A heads can be all caps, flush left, two line spaces above and one line space below. If there is an outline number or letter, that should be used as part of the A head.

1. BACKGROUND

This is the general appearance of an A head with an outline number. The main points in a report are A-head titles.

B heads can be upper- and lowercase, flush left, one line space above and one line space below. B heads are used for divisions of thought and text within a main point and are subordinate to the A head.

a. Company Experience to the Present

This is the general appearance of a B head with an outline letter. B heads are subsections of material in a main section. Usually, there are two or more B heads under a single A head if the material in the A-head section is divided into smaller sections.

C heads can be upper- and lowercase, beginning with an indent from the left margin, one line space above and one line space below. C heads are used for subsections within a B-head section.

i. Company Experience: 1945–75

This is the general appearance of a C head. In such a development of material, a second C head might carry the historical analysis further.

ii. Company Experience: 1976–85

D heads can be upper- and lowercase, underlined or italics (if you have a word processor or an italics typing element for your typewriter), beginning with an indent from the left margin, one line space above and one line space below. D heads are seldom used since they are subsections of subsections of subsections. Unless the report is carefully structured and very complex with a clear outline, the significance of D heads can readily be overlooked by the casual reader.

(a) *Experience: 1976–85—Atlanta*
(b) *Experience: 1976–85—Houston*
(c) *Experience: 1976–85—Denver*

These three D heads suggest how a report might break down an analysis in some detail, based on regional centers or marketing centers, or product lines, depending on the nature of the company and the purpose of the report.

4. Contents

After the report is completed, with page numbers, prepare a table of contents, using the A-, B-, C-, and D-head titles as the titles in the table of contents. Indent each level of heads. The page number can follow each entry by three spaces or it can be flush right at the end of the entry. If the entry is two or more lines, the page number should be on the last line of the entry. A sample contents page follows. The contents page usually is placed immediately after the executive summary, or after the title page, if there is no executive summary.

Sample Contents Page of a Report

If the final report is typed single-spaced, it may appear too crowded unless there are frequent heads to break up the feeling of close-typed, wall-to-wall copy. If it is typed double-spaced, it may appear to be too open and seem to be too long for easy reading since it takes up so many sheets of paper. Sometimes the best solution is to use one-and-a-half-line spacing. This is easy to read and is more condensed than double spacing.

Draft copies of the report, however, should be typed doubled-spaced—or even triple-spaced, if your equipment has that capability—so your boss can easily edit, adjust, rewrite, and add.

In today's office, a report that will require text manipulation and change before the final copy is prepared should be entered into a word-processing system. Even if you do not have one yourself, have your boss make arrangements with the appropriate people in the company so that versions of the report are done on a word processor. This not only saves much retyping, but it ensures that new errors are not continually introduced into the report during the process of constant retyping of sections of the report.

A report should have numbered pages. The numbers can be placed at the center top or bottom of each page. Or they can be flushed to the right at the top, with the name of the report or with the name of the section of the report:

TOWN OF SQUANTUM: Water Resources / 6

For the first page of the report, the page number is often centered at the bottom of the page, even though all the following pages have the numbers in the upper right-hand corners.

To make the most professional impression, the report should be placed in a presentation folder. These are sometimes folders with three-hole clasps. Sometimes a plastic gripper is placed along the left-hand side of the folder, and sometimes a plastic comb binding can be used to dress up the presentation and ensure the report is given extra attention. If a report is worth the executive time to prepare, and the secretarial time to produce, it can be worth a few more cents to call attention to its importance by dressing it in a presentation folder.

CHAPTER 16
FINANCIAL STATEMENTS

Depending on your boss's role in the company, you may have to type financial statements from time to time. If you have a word processor or have access to one, these statements are far easier to prepare. Mistakes are easier to correct in word processing, and it is impossible to get every figure absolutely right in a complex financial statement.

An even greater benefit of word-processing financial statements is the ability to retain the format and to copy data without having to retype it (thus avoiding introducing new typos while retyping). Usually in a financial statement, last year's figures for the same period are shown alongside this year's figures. It is easy on a word-processing system to make "this year's" figures into "last year's" figures when you add a new set of "this year's" figures, provided you kept the diskette for financial statements. You delete the old figures, move the present figures for this year into the last year's column, and add the new this year's figures. In word processing, you retain the overall format and one half of the figures you need; you have only to add the new figures for the period being reported.

Financial statements are usually prepared

quarterly. Annual figures are included in the company's annual report.

Usually there are two sections to financial statements. One is the "profit-and-loss" or "income-and-expenditure" summary of monies received and monies spent during the period being reported. The second is a "balance sheet," or statement of present worth. The profit and loss, usually abbreviated P/L, is a historical record over a period of time. The balance sheet is a kind of snapshot of total worth at the moment the picture is taken.

Reporting periods may include quarterly and annual (three- and twelve-month) periods. In some summaries, the history may go back longer than the same period last year if long-term trends are being studied or presented.

A sample of each kind of financial statement follows. Your company's financial statements will differ somewhat in that accounting practices may differ and the nature of your company's business will call for different categories. But, by and large, the same general kinds of categories will appear.

In a P/L statement there is a recording of the source of income to the company, the kinds of expenditures made, and whether there was an overall profit or loss for the reporting period. Here is a P/L statement, showing last year, this year, and amount of increase or decrease.

STATEMENT OF CONSOLIDATED INCOME

	This year	Last year	Increase *Decrease*
	(In Thousands)		
Net Sales	$1,792,938	$1,637,482	$155,456
Cost of Goods Sold.............................	1,324,595	1,214,561	110,034
Gross Profit	468,343	422,921	45,422
Less:			
Selling and administrative expenses	179,611	162,779	16,832
Research, development, patent and engineering expenses .	86,281	84,224	2,057
	265,892	247,003	18,889
Operating Profit	202,451	175,918	26,533
Income Charges—Net	11,519	10,445	1,074
Income Before Income Taxes	190,932	165,473	25,459
Provision for Income Taxes:			
Current	83,908	70,238	13,670
Deferred (credit)	(1,801)	(3,462)	1,661
	82,107	66,776	15,331
Income Before Extraordinary Item	108,825	98,697	10,128
Extraordinary Gain on Sale of Investment, Less Applicable Income Tax of $2,131,000...........		6,394	*6,394*
Net Income.....................................	$ 108,825	$ 105,091	$ 3,734

In a balance sheet, there is a summary of assets (things or money the company has, or money that is owed to the company), liabilities (obligations the company has to others), and net worth (the difference between the assets and the liabilities). If, for instance, a company has assets of $100,000, but owes $35,000, the net worth of the company is $65,000. Sometimes the net worth is called stockholders' or owners' equity, meaning how much the company would be worth to them after all the bills are paid. Here is a sample balance sheet.

CONSOLIDATED BALANCE SHEET

December 31	This year	Last year
Assets		
Current assets		
Cash	$ 12,622,000	$ 10,623,000
Marketable securities, at cost which approximates market value	1,793,000	1,142,000
Accounts receivable, less reserve: This year, $778,000; Last year, $616,000	52,873,000	38,313,000
Inventories	47,461,000	43,410,000
Other current assets and prepayments	6,729,000	3,114,000
Total current assets	121,478,000	96,602,000
Capital assets	82,194,000	73,928,000
Patents and goodwill, less amortization	2,207,000	2,763,000
Other assets	2,225,000	1,713,000
Total assets	$208,104,000	$175,006,000

	This year	Last year
Liabilities and stockholders' equity		
Current liabilities		
Accounts payable	$ 24,973,000	$ 18,828,000
Income taxes payable	7,498,000	886,000
Notes payable and current portion of long-term debt	6,210,000	15,116,000
Advance billings	17,876,000	15,842,000
Total current liabilities	56,557,000	50,672,000
Deferred taxes on income	5,344,000	6,156,000
Long-term debt	34,453,000	15,724,000
Total liabilities	96,354,000	72,552,000
Stockholders' equity		
4% convertible cumulative preferred stock, $50 par value	12,000,000	12,000,000
Common stock, $2 par value	11,973,000	11,922,000
Capital in excess of par value	19,743,000	18,517,000
Retained earnings	68,034,000	60,015,000
Total stockholders' equity	111,750,000	102,454,000
Total liabilities and stockholders' equity	$208,104,000	$175,006,000

My purpose in showing you these forms is not to teach accounting or how to read a financial statement. (You may become interested in reading a financial statement and learn how to recognize when your company is in trouble and you should be looking elsewhere, but that is a by-product of working in the preparation of these statements.) This section of *Secretarial Practice Made Simple* is simply to alert you to the general appearance of these statements and to indicate their general contents. They summarize your company's activity—and disclose whether the company has made any money—so they are of great interest to company executives, board members, stockholders, and the general financial public. Accuracy and a pleasing appearance are essential in a company's financial statements.

CHAPTER 17
MEETINGS

If your boss is responsible for conducting committee meetings, part of your work will be to assist him in preparing for the meetings and following up after the meetings. These responsibilities may include physical arrangements for the meeting itself, depending on where it is held.

AGENDA

In preparation for the meeting, an agenda—or list of topics to be considered—has to be set down. Along with this is the determination of who should attend the meeting. If it is an established committee, those attending include the members of the committee, any specially invited guests or experts, and any company staff who normally or by special invitation are to sit in on this committee. You will have a list of the committee members and regular staff attendees. Your boss will add any special guests and any other company staff who should be at this meeting.

Once the agenda is set by your boss and the list of attendees is determined, you should send out an announcement of the meeting together with a copy of the agenda. The announcement should include date, time, and place, together with an address and telephone number to call in case they are unable to attend or to confirm their attendance. Confirmation of attendance is important if food is to be served in connection with the meeting or if the meeting is to be held at a location that requires hotel reservations. The notice of the meeting with the agenda should be sent sufficiently ahead of the day of the meeting so that everyone feels he has been given a fair chance to consider the topics and prepare, at least in part, for the meeting. Two weeks is usually accepted as sufficient. Some meetings, such as stockholders meetings, have a legal requirement that those invited receive notice a specific number of days before the meeting.

TIP

In preparation for a meeting, an agenda—or list of topics to be considered—has to be set down.

REPORTS AND FINANCIAL STATEMENTS

Certain items on the agenda will call for reports or financial statements to be presented at the meeting for discussion. Part of your boss's responsibility for the meeting is to see that these reports and financial statements or statistical summaries are prepared in advance of the meeting and are presented in handout or audiovisual form at the meeting. Therefore part of your job will be to put those reports and statements in the form he wishes, or to ensure that that is done.

These reports are formal company documents, and they will assume a standard format. They are then kept as part of the record of the work of that committee and as part of the archives of the company. Care in their preparation is essential. Give yourself adequate time to proofread them so that neither you nor your boss is embarrassed by some committee member pointing out typos. If your financial reports are not computer printouts, be sure to add each column of figures so that some committee member who is keeping himself mentally occupied during the meeting by adding the columns does not catch your boss in an arithmetic error and thus cloud his credibility on the points he is trying to make.

PHYSICAL ARRANGEMENTS

You need to ensure the meeting is fully prepared for in physical arrangements. The best way to ensure that everything is planned for in advance is to develop a checklist that you run through for each meeting. Every once in a while something will come up that you had not foreseen. Even though you cannot provide for it for that particular meeting, add the item to your meeting checklist to make sure it does not come up a second time.

A Checklist for a Meeting at the Company

A meeting checklist should contain the following items, as well as those required by your boss, your special circumstances, and your experience:

1. Reserve the meeting room.
2. Personally check the room before the meeting to ensure:
   a. There are enough chairs.
   b. The room is clean.
   c. There are water and glasses at convenient locations on the table.
   d. There are notepads and pencils for each chair.
   e. There are sufficient ashtrays on the table.
   f. The room is at the right temperature.
   g. Name cards are placed, if desired.
   h. Required audiovisual equipment is on hand and working.
   i. A podium is on hand, if desired, and any loudspeaker system works.

3. Make sure security and the receptionist know the meeting is scheduled and know where to direct people who come from outside the company.
4. If eating is part of the meeting schedule, whether a lunch or a coffee break with rolls and pastry or afternoon drinks, make sure catering and serving arrangements are under control.
5. If there are exhibits to be passed around during the meeting, make sure they are on hand.

A Checklist for a Meeting Outside the Company

If the meeting is held outside the company at a hotel or conference center, there are further complications and your meeting checklist needs to include:

6. Transportation arrangements to and from the location.
7. Room reservations for all who are staying over, including who will room with whom if rooms are to be shared.

8. Meal arrangements, including menu selection if there is a meal in a private dining room.
9. Payment arrangements, permitting those attending to sign for room and meal charges.
10. Posting of the meeting schedule and location.
11. Retrieval to the office of unused and undistributed materials.

Since your boss is responsible for the running of the meeting or its arrangements, you will need to go over this checklist with him to give specific content to many of the items. You should also give him a typed copy of the final checklist, with all details noted, so he will have an answer at hand if he is asked about any particular. Or he will know what was not foreseen and planned for if something unexpected comes up. His on-the-spot decision-making will be better when he sees clearly all the decisions that were made as part of the planning of the meeting.

IF YOU ATTEND THE MEETING

If you attend the meeting, whether in the company or outside, part of your responsibility is to see that all runs smoothly according to plan and with as little attention drawn to the mechanics of the meeting as possible. The important reason for the meeting is the accomplishment of the business on the agenda. The smoother and less obviously the physical arrangements are handled the more the attendees will concentrate on the business and not on the physical arrangements.

TIP

Drop a short note of thanks to key people whose help made the meeting run smoothly.

MINUTES OF THE MEETING

While the meeting is taking place, some record will probably have to be kept. The nature of these minutes or proceedings will vary from company to company and meeting to meeting. Your boss may ask you to "take minutes." If so, clarify with him beforehand how extensive a record he wants. Perhaps the best way at first—until you come to a mutual understanding of what is desired—is to make notations around the topics listed on the agenda that will serve as a basis for him to dictate what he wants as a record of the meeting. Your notations will serve as reminders of what was discussed. Much of what is said will probably be left unreported; much of it is repetitious or not to the point. Your boss will have a good sense of what should be retained from the discussion as he reviews your "memory jogger" notes.

If a formal resolution is passed, you should record it word for word at the meeting. Time is often spent at the meeting agreeing on exact wording, and the people at the meeting will be grateful when you persist in making sure those exact words are in your notes.

For note-taking at a meeting, shorthand can be useful. However, it is not essential. You can develop your own abbreviation system. Apart from formal resolutions, you generally do not need verbatim accounts or records. You need to listen and to summarize the gist of what is being said. A business meeting is not a court of law in which a court reporter has to take down every hem and haw as well as every word. The report or minutes of the meeting will serve as a general record of what took place and this record often serves as a point of reference for new directions and improved performance by company employees.

FOLLOW-UP AFTER THE MEETING

The final matter to handle after the meeting is over and the record has been prepared is to send out any material that was promised to those who attended the meeting or was decided upon by those at the meeting to send to others. Those who attended the meeting, as well as certain other executives in the company, should receive a copy of the proceedings. This will give them a chance to get in touch with your boss if they feel some important matter was left out or was not quite correctly recorded. It will also inform executives in the company what took place, even though they were not there. Your boss will determine who is on the "for your information" list to receive a copy of the proceedings.

You should also drop a short note of thanks to key people whose help made the meeting run smoothly. Some of these notes should be in your boss's name; others can be in yours. People who have been thanked for doing their job well will try even harder the next time. People whose hard work is taken for granted tend to be less and less committed as time goes on.

TIP

After the meeting is over and the immediate post-meeting tasks done, review the arrangements with your boss to determine how the next meeting can be even better.

THE NEXT MEETING

After the meeting is over and the immediate post-meeting tasks done, review the arrangements with your boss to determine how the next meeting can be even better. Use your checklist as the agenda for the review, and develop a modified checklist for the next meeting in the light of your experience with the meeting just past. There are consulting firms whose sole business is arranging meetings for companies. Read their books and announcements for ideas; keep your eyes open for new ideas as you attend meetings conducted by others. Thorough and smooth meeting arranging is an excellent skill for career advancement.

CHAPTER 18

FILING

"Please bring the file on the Johnson account when you come." "The file" is almost a magical incantation in the office. Whenever some detail is forgotten or some agreement needs to be reviewed or some question arises about a matter, "the file" is read to find the answer.

The file contains pieces of paper: copies of incoming and outgoing correspondence, copies of orders, statements of accounts, shipping documents, copies of memos, handwritten notes summarizing a telephone conversation, memos to the file. It contains a running record of relationships, agreements, and controversies with other parties. If a critical piece is missing—or never was created—the file cannot provide the answer that is sought. If everything is there, the file provides the background for making the next decision about an ongoing business relationship.

THE KEEPER OF THE FILE

The file is generated by activity between your boss and her business colleagues. You are its keeper. You determine what goes in. You have to answer for it if crucial papers are missing. You have to be able to put your hands on the file at a moment's notice. You have to know where the file is at any moment—on your boss's desk, in her briefcase, at her home, on your desk, in the file drawer, on the typist's desk. And you have to know how this file relates to others on related subjects.

THE FILE AS AN ONGOING RECORD

Very seldom in a career does a secretary have the job of creating a system of files. There are many different filing systems, each fraught with benefits and disadvantages. Since you usually inherit an ongoing filing system, I will not spend time and effort discussing possible filing systems you might install if you had the opportunity. Only once in about four decades

---

TIP

Usually you have to work with a filing system that has had many secretaries and many bosses, that has sometimes benefited from them and sometimes suffered from them, and that will undoubtedly outlast both you and your boss.

---

of office work did I have the opportunity to set up the files the way I thought they should be, and that was when I established my own company. And even then my partner got into the act in ways I thought were less than perfect. So, you have to work with a filing system that has had many secretaries and many bosses, that has sometimes benefited from them and sometimes suffered from them, and will undoubtedly outlast both you and your boss in that department.

As you maintain your files, keep in mind those who will follow you. Will they be able to find what they are looking for? It is no compliment to be the only person who can find something in your files. Even your boss may have to look for something sometime when you are ill or she is working on a Sunday.

LEARN THE FILES

Read each one as you have need of it. Read other files in the early days on the job before you are so busy that you do not have the leisure to browse through them. When you add to one, see how what you add relates to what occurred before. When correspondence comes in from someone and you pull the file to send in with the correspondence to your boss, glance through the file to get a feeling for the subject and the people.

RESPECT THE FILES

At first, put more into the file than not. In time, you will develop a feel for what is significant and should be filed and what is trivial and need not be filed. But when you begin working with a file, err on the side of filing too much. You can always clean out the trivia at a later time, but you can never reconstruct data that has been thrown away hastily.

INTRODUCE ANY CHANGES
TO THE FILES
SLOWLY AND CAUTIOUSLY

The system has worked somehow until now. Your concept of how they should be organized may be superficially sound, but may have serious flaws for the long haul. Make changes in the files only after you have been in the job long enough to know that your modifications to the system would be a true improvement, that those who inherit your files would inherit a better working system than you inherited. You should make only minor changes, here and there, improving not radically restructuring the files. To make major changes in the filing system is a major task that will keep you from other activities for months. Is the end result for all that time and effort and distraction from other activity worth it? Usually not.

HOUSEKEEPING

Do housekeeping on the files, but do it only after you know what is important. It takes several months on the job to have a perspective on the pieces of paper that make up the file. After you have served that apprenticeship in this job, you should review each file as you need it and throw away trivia that has collected in the file. Memos and letters about meeting dates long since past need no longer take up file space. If accounting keeps records of data, there are copies of that data in the file, and those copies are long outdated, they can be tossed out. But anything that looks as though it has any long-term value should be kept. You may decide ten months from now, when you next pull the file and review its contents, that a particular piece of paper can go, but better to make that decision later than sooner. The balance to be struck is somewhere between being a pack rat that collects and stores everything and a careless destroyer of information that will have value in the months or years ahead. Perhaps the key is to save too much at the beginning, and throw much of it out during later reviews of the file.

ORIGINALS OF CONTRACTS AND AGREEMENTS

Originals of contracts and formal agreements are best kept in a secure alternative filing location or in a separate folder, but keep a copy of the original in the working file with a notation where the original is kept. The originals are legal documents, often of considerable worth to the company and very difficult, if not impossible, to duplicate if lost. I usually stapled the copies of such documents to the file folder so that even a copy would not be inadvertently discarded.

Regarding copies of financial reports and records that are sent to your boss from ac-counting or the treasurer's office, your boss need keep those copies only so long as they are useful management tools to her. The company's official record copies are maintained elsewhere in the company. Work out with your boss an understanding of how long she estimates she might need these reports in her own work. Keep them at least that long—perhaps a quarter longer—and then throw them out. If she ever needs a copy a year or two later, she can request a copy from the originating office.

CONFIDENTIAL INFORMATION

If you are throwing away confidential information as you maintain the files, use a shredder or tear the material into two or four pieces. Many companies view their financial records as confidential, and those records should not be thrown undestroyed into the trash. Your boss can guide you regarding company policy on what is confidential and how those records are to be destroyed when they are no longer needed.

TIP

It is not a compliment to be known as the only person who can find something in your files.

SPACE FOR FILES

Files and file maintenance cost money. The files themselves take space—valuable space that the company pays for by the square foot annually. Additional file drawers are expensive. The time for a file clerk or the use of your time to keep the files current and to ac-

cess them is much more costly now than it was years ago. Therefore, the efforts you give to keeping the size and growth of the files under control is of great value to the company.

MICROFILMING FILES

In many companies, the expense for space and mushrooming files is so great that they have adopted the policy of microfilming them. The file is photographed and reduced to the size of a large postage stamp. It can be read only with an enlarging device; often photocopies can be made so you or your boss can have a hard copy. These miniature copies are either on a roll of film or are assembled on a card called a microfiche. Valuable original documents are preserved, normal file contents are microfilmed and kept at a central repository or library, and this year's working file is maintained by you in your office. You may send down an old file every so often for microfilming.

If you are ever in an office that converts to microfilming while you are there, you will go through a nightmarish year or two while your older files are processed. If, however, you come into an office where microfilming is a standard practice, you have only to learn what the pattern is and adapt to it.

Your boss cannot retrieve microfilmed files as readily as she can your current file. It takes time for the file archivist to locate the microfilm, copy what is needed, and send it to you. Depending on the situation and the urgency, it may take hours or weeks.

ELECTRONIC FILES

If your office is wired into a computer mainframe, and if you or your boss have a terminal that has access to the mainframe, you may file some of your records electronically. You would be able to call them up on your terminal—and that may suffice for you to get the

information you want. Or you may call the record up and then print it out so that you can give your boss a hard copy.

Data records—finances, orders, bills, and the like—have been maintained in computer data banks for many years. Increasingly, written business records are also being maintained in computer data banks. These are usually called "information systems" or "electronic filing systems." The detailed means of using these systems and gaining access to their contents depends in great measure on the equipment your company has secured.

What you do with an electronic file is really no different from what you do with a paper file; *how* you do it will be different, since it

will be done by use of a keyboard instead of opening a drawer across the room. You will still have to learn the files, respect them, introduce changes very slowly, and perform routine housekeeping on them. And you will still have to retrieve them for the boss, either by "sending" them to her terminal, if she has one, or by getting a printout of a document that is related to the matter at hand.

FILES AND THE FILE CLERK

You may be your own file clerk, or you may have a file clerk working for you. That file clerk may work full-time for you or serve several secretaries from a centralized file area. If you have a file clerk, you should never become so dependent on that person that you are paralyzed when that person is sick or is on vacation. You should be able to find your way

around your own files when the file clerk is busy on some other assignment. Don't let your file clerk take over your files; remember that he works for you. If he knows that you know what he does about the files, you will be able to keep control of his work. A slipshod file clerk can do you and your boss in very quickly.

CROSS-REFERENCING FILES

Cross-reference filing may sound impressive in books about filing, but I have found attempts at cross-reference filing to result in more confusion and lead to greater loss of effective working time than in any positive gains. It is much easier just to take a photo-

copy of a document and put a copy in each place where you think it belongs—indicating on the copy where the master is filed (remember to remove the copies when they are no longer needed).

TIP

Make changes in the files only after you have been in the job long enough to know that your modifications to the system would be a true improvement.

FILING SUGGESTIONS

Some standard filing suggestions are worth repeating; they are sound and are based on proven practice:

1. File correspondence files by alphabet, with the most recent date on top.

2. File subject files according to a pattern that makes good sense in your office, breaking a subject into sub-subjects only when there seems good reason to do so.

3. Staple pieces of related correspondence together.

4. Do not use paper clips in a file to hold paper together.

5. Most recent papers are filed on top, and they work down through time in reverse to the back of the file.

6. If someone takes (or is sent) part of a file, a piece of paper containing a brief description of what was sent, when, and to whom is dropped into the file. You never know when you might need to track it down.

No file is ever in perfect condition. Every file is always in a state of change. Remember that the files exist for the sake of the job being done; the workers do not exist to maintain files. Make the files produce for you and your boss; you will learn what is expected from them as the job goes on. For the files to produce what you want when you want it will take careful and regular attention on your part, but the end result of an easy, working filing system is a better and easier job for you. Be pragmatic about your files, not perfectionistic. Devote as much attention to them as they need, but no more. Use your other time for career development in other aspects of your job.

PART IV

LETTER AND MEMO SKILLS

Much of your work as a secretary is preparing letters, memos, and reports. I include in Part IV a broad sweep of details that have helped me do a more professional job in writing letters and memos and in preparing company reports.

There are many details contained in some of the books that can aid you in a particular field. If, for instance, you become a secretary in a naval office, you will need to know how to address officers of various grades and how to write a "Navy letter." The Department of the Navy has prepared correspondence handbooks that contain titles, addresses and forms of address, and Navy letter characteristics. There is no need to go into that kind of detail here: If you are not in a naval office, the information is of little use to you; if you are in a naval office, it is needless repetition.

Likewise, if you are a secretary in a Roman Catholic chancery, you need to learn all the titles and proper forms of address for several varieties of clergy (from Pope to novitiate), nuns, and brothers. These titles and forms are readily available in every chancery office; in an Episcopalian diocese's office, the titles and forms of address are noticeably different, and even more so if you work in a Baptist convention office.

The letter, memo, and report skills I develop in this section are useful in whatever kind of corporation or institution you work in. These suggestions are general in nature; you will have to fill in around them with all the specific styles, titles, and forms that are used in your situation.

CHAPTER 19
GRAMMAR AND SENTENCE STRUCTURE

For much of your transcribing work, you will have little to do with the final wording of what you type. Your boss has dictated what he wants to have written, and that is that. However, depending on the way you and your boss work out the nature of your job, you may increasingly have the opportunity to write letters and reports on your own.

This book is not a detailed guide to grammar, spelling, usage, and writing. There are many excellent books readily available to meet those needs. You may wish to add them to your professional bookshelf for ready reference. Here, however, are some general suggestions for business writing:

1. *Write in the active rather than the passive voice*. Instead of saying "It is desired that . . ." (passive voice), say "We hope that . . ." (active voice). Or instead of saying "It is requested that you send . . ." (passive voice), say "Please send . . ." (active voice).

The passive voice is weak as well as impersonal. Often business and government executives have been indoctrinated with the idea that they should not intrude their own personality into business correspondence, and therefore they use the passive extensively. If your boss is thoroughly conditioned in this way, he will undoubtedly feel comfortable only when he cannot be seen behind the flood of words it takes to phrase everything in a passive manner.

But increasingly business executives are urged in business schools and government workers are urged in writing style memos to express themselves actively and personally in

---

TIP

Most business readers will glance at your letter in the middle of a busy, work-filled day, grasp its main point if it clearly stands out, and skim over the rest.

their correspondence. If your boss is attempting to be more direct in his correspondence and has also turned over to you the writing of standard routine replies, think "active" when you write your letters.

2. *Make your paragraph a unit of thought.* A paragraph should contain one main idea. That idea is expressed or summed up in one sentence in the paragraph. The other sentences in the paragraph help introduce the idea or give a fuller explanation of it or provide reasons to support it. If you start to introduce a second main idea, you should create another paragraph for that idea.

In business correspondence, a paragraph can sometimes consist of a single sentence. Most paragraphs, however, take more than one sentence, because the writer wants to fill in his idea with further detail.

Just as a business letter should normally have one subject, which can be highlighted for easy reference and filing, so each paragraph should have one idea about the subject, which can be underlined for rapid scanning.

Usually, you write more clearly if the first sentence of the paragraph contains the main idea. The reader does not have to search throughout the paragraph for clues about what you consider important. The point of business correspondence is to be clear, direct, uncomplicated. To hide the main idea somewhere in the middle of the paragraph complicates the process of interpreting what you mean and how forthrightly you mean it.

If a paragraph builds on the idea of the previous paragraph, you help the reader make the transition by using such words or phrases as "therefore," "however," "as we said before," and so on.

You should consider how long a paragraph should be. Your reader will tend to get lost in a very long paragraph, even though it has only one main idea. You can help the reader who might otherwise get lost in a very long paragraph by breaking it into two or three shorter paragraphs at points where the content takes a step forward in its development.

Not only can a reader become lost in too long a paragraph, but he can also be distracted by a series of very short paragraphs. The reader needs time—and material in the paragraph to fill in an idea with some content—to take in and think over that idea a little before having another one thrust upon him.

Remember that most business readers will glance at your letter in the middle of a busy, work-filled day, grasp its main point if it clearly stands out, and skim over the rest. Your skill in crafting a letter that contains the main ideas in an obvious position and in clear language will aid them as they attempt to understand what you want to communicate to them.

3. *Do away with needless words.* Most business letters could have up to half their words taken out and the letters would be better letters. This is especially true of dictated letters. A dictator often rambles as he tries to come up with the best way to express an idea.

TIP

Positive statements are usually more concise than negative circumlocutions.

He may even rephrase the idea in two or three different sentences in his search for the best way to communicate it. If he were writing the letter by hand or on a typewriter, he would probably delete the less successful attempts. But now they are on the tape, and it is too much trouble to go back over and redictate now that he has come up with the wording he wants. So the "thinking out loud" flavor remains in the letter.

If this is an important letter, you and your boss may have a standing agreement that you can type out a double-spaced draft so he can go through the body of the letter and tighten it up.

This does not mean that every sentence has to be short. It means that unnecessary words should be struck out.

For instance, "there is no question but that . . ." can become "without question." "This is a matter that" becomes "This matter." "Dedicated to transportation purposes" might be "used for transportation." "Owing to the fact that" is better simply as "since." And "call your attention to the fact that" can be "notify you" or "remind you."

Positive statements are usually more concise than negative circumlocutions: "It is not without reason that" should be "it is reasonable that" or "my reason for." And "the loss for the fourth quarter was not inconsiderable in the light of general economic trends" might be "our fourth-quarter loss was greater than expected given general economic trends."

You should not make the recipient read a sentence over and over again to figure out what you are trying to say, however subtly you are trying to phrase your point. In business correspondence, he should be able to get your meaning clearly in one reading. Unnecessary words make it harder for him to unravel your meaning.

4. *Keep an eye out for misplaced antecedents.* An antecedent is something connected that precedes, and in grammar it refers to the word, phrase, or clause to which a relative pronoun refers. A relative pronoun is the "who," "which," "it," "that," or "they" in a sentence such as "He who laughs last laughs best." "He" is the antecedent of "who" in that sentence.

It is very easy in a long, complex sentence—especially when it is being dictated—to separate the antecedent and its relative pronoun by so many ideas and words that the relative pronoun (with its accompanying clause) gets attached to the wrong antecedent. This results in confusion or ludicrous phrases.

"The captain of the ship with the two stacks that sailed illegally into New York harbor was called up to a court of inquiry" raises the image of two smokestacks sailing into the harbor. In this sentence, "ship" is the proper antecedent for "that sailed into New York harbor." But because "with the two stacks" gets placed between the rightful antecedent and its connected relative pronoun, the clear sense intended got muddled.

The rule of thumb is that a relative pronoun and its clause should follow immediately or as close as possible after the word it is related to. Whenever you see a relative pronoun, look back to the word it follows to see if the sentence makes straightforward sense. Adjust the sentence or divide it so that it makes straightforward sense. "The captain of the ship—the one with two stacks—that sailed illegally into New York harbor was called up to a court of inquiry." Or "The captain of the ship that sailed illegally into New York harbor was called up to a court of inquiry. His ship was a two-stacker." Or "The captain was called up to a court of inquiry for sailing his ship, which has two stacks, illegally into New York harbor."

TIP

Your ear for normal, standard English is to be trusted. Listening to the sound and sense of the sentence will help you avoid stilted expressions.

"The snow fell for two days on the house and it melted." The sun has to be especially hot to melt a house. A better way of expressing the idea would be, "After falling on the house for two days, the snow melted." "The contracts were sent to both parties, and they were not legal" is the same kind of misplaced antecedent. The writer means to say that the contracts were not properly drawn up rather than meaning to cast aspersions on the ethics of the contracting parties. The sentence could be rewritten "The contracts were sent in all good faith to both parties. However, careful reading showed that the documents were incorrectly drawn up." Or, "The contracts, which were not legally prepared, were sent to both parties."

5. *Think more about how a sentence sounds than about following strict rules of grammar.* Your ear for normal, standard English is to be trusted. Not only have you learned standard English in school, but you hear it every day on radio and television. News programs and documentaries especially use educated—but not pretentious—language

in an easy, flowing manner. Your ear would be jarred if Dan Rather misused the language, for example, by saying "they wasn't," even though you might be at a loss to describe instantly in grammatical terms what was wrong.

It is quite permissible to split an infinitive ("to carefully decide after studying all sides of the problem"), to end a sentence with a preposition ("I need some petty cash to pay the bills with."), and to use "me" instead of "I" in such phrases as "if anyone should represent the company at the meeting, it's me." "I" may be formally correct, but "me" strikes the ear as normal.

Listening to the sound and sense of the sentence will help you avoid stilted expressions. Equally, you will readily sense that some expressions might sound too breezy or slangy for a business letter. Such breeziness results from a desire to draw attention to yourself; it's as though you are saying, "Look at me—look how clever I am." And when you do that, the reader is so distracted by his opinions of your attempted cleverness that he may never focus on the point of the correspondence.

CHAPTER 20

SPELLING

It is well known that English is one of the difficult languages to spell. It is not consistently phonetic; that is, every written consonant and vowel does not always represent the same sound. "G" is sometimes a hard sound, as in "gruff"; it is sometimes a soft sound, as in "gem"; it is sometimes used with other consonants to represent an "f-type" sound, as in "enough"; and sometimes it is in the spelling, but represents no sound at all, as in "bough."

The English language has developed from many languages, borrowing words and phrases from all. Rooted in early Anglo-Saxon, mixed with Celtic and Latin, then Norman, and borrowing heavily from Greek, French, German, Norse, and Arabic, this complex language has been richly seasoned by Spanish, Chinese, Japanese, American Indian, and numerous African languages. In each case, words that have entered arrived with their original spelling and pronunciation. In time the pronunciation changed to be more in conformity with developing tones of English, whereas the spelling tended to remain in the native form. This has created all kinds of so-called inconsistencies in our language that purists from time to time try, without success,

to correct. We are slow (not "slo") to accept linguistic changes, even though we are quick to invent informal language and borrow elements from other languages when it is useful to do so.

Many English spellings reflect the sounds that were once part of the word when it was first used in the language: In "night" the "gh" was once pronounced as a kind of guttural consonant in the back of the throat, similar to such sounds in German today. That consonant was lost in English, but the spelling lingers on. "Nite" is still ad-speak, not everyday, accepted English. The same is true of "high"; but we still accept "hiway" only in traffic signs where there is a need to use as few letters as possible. This is also true of "through" and "thruway."

Other English spellings reflect the standard spelling in the language from which it was borrowed: "Petit" is from French and means "small" or "tiny" or "minor." But in English, it is pronounced the same as "petty," which generally means "trivial" or "trifling" or "insignificant." Thus, there are "petit juries" as compared with "grand juries"; "petit point" (involving intricate, detailed needlework); and "petit fours" (small, rich tea cakes). You need to know the difference between "petit" and "petty" to use the correct spelling. Indeed, some juries can be petty, as well as petit.

Plurals often present a spelling problem, since the plural form is usually related to the language from which the word was borrowed. In some words, the plural is the same as the singular: "Marquis" is both singular and plural, although some English writers have given the English-style plural to the word in the form of "marquises." So now both "marquis" and "marquises" are correct English plurals for the singular "marquis." In other words, the plural is based on the original language in its construction: "Index" is "indices" according to the Latin original. And many writers still use this form. However, many are using the English-style form of "indexes."

In certain words borrowed from Greek, the singular ends in "um" and the plural in "a." Thus, a "phylum" is a major division of the animal kingdom in scientific terms. Several such divisions are "phyla." However, this is not a hard-and-fast rule. A scientific word borrowed from Greek is "pseudopodium." It basically means "false foot" and refers to certain one-celled animals, such as an amoeba, that advance a part of their protoplasm to encircle and absorb a speck of food or to move from one place to another (the animal flows into the part it sent out, drawing the rest of itself into the new location, and then sends out a new pseudopodium to continue its movement). More than one of these "false feet" are "pseudopodia." So far, this follows the "phylum-phyla" pattern for Greek words; however, the singular of "pseudopodia" now often is "pseudopod" and the plural of "pseudopod" increasingly is seen in the work of some writers as "pseudopods."

For purists, the singular for "media" is "medium." Thus, TV is a "medium," but TV and newspapers are "media." However, in popular usage "medium" sounds stilted in many sentences where it is really proper: "Could anyone ever replace Walter Cronkite as a medium personality?" The singular of "data" is "datum." Most people outside of the scientific community now use "data" as both the singular and plural form.

Accurate spelling is a matter of early drill work in school. The more you know of other languages, the more you will understand spelling patterns and variances. Accurate spelling can be achieved and developed by frequent use of a dictionary and a speller wordbook.

A speller wordbook (usually called a "speller-divider" since it also includes word-division breaks) is a simple alphabetical listing—without definition—of thousands of words. A good speller book will have about 50,000 words. It shows not only the spelling of the main word, but also derivatives and alternate spellings:

me-chan-ic

me-chan-i-cal

me-chan-i-cal-ly

me-chan-ics

mech-a-nism

mech-a-nis-tic

mech-a-nis-ti-cal-ly

mech-a-ni-za-tion

mech-a-nize

mech-a-nized

mech-a-niz-ing

Or:

fo-cal

fo-cal-ly

fo-cus

pl. fo-cus-es or fo-ci

v. fo-cused or fo-cussed

    fo-cus-ing or fo-cus-sing

There are no definitions, but there are complete spelling patterns for every generally used word in English.

If your work calls for extensive legal language, there are spellers for legal terms. The same is true for medical terms. These wordbooks or spellers are available from any well-stocked reference section in a bookstore or office-supply store. Whenever you have the least doubt about how to spell a word, look it up in your speller. You will find the speller much easier and faster to use than a dictionary. The dictionary is essential when you need to know the meaning of a word, or when you need to decide which word to use where alternatives can be easily confused. If you are uncertain whether to use ''proceed'' or ''precede,'' you need to go to your dictionary to determine which is the proper word for the context in which you are using it. The speller will not help you resolve that question. However, if you know the proper word is ''proceed,'' the speller will remind you not to misspell it ''procede.''

There are some problem spelling areas that it is helpful to be aware of. If you are prone to make mistakes in any of the areas, take extra care to use your speller when you encounter a word in one of your problem areas. In time, you will find that particular word no longer a problem; but if you do not use it for a long time, it may be a problem again when you meet it.

Problem spelling areas include:

1. Words that end in *-ence* or *-ance, -ent* or *-ant*. Keep using your speller. Even when you feel positive about a spelling, you can be mistaken.

2. When to make a plural by adding *-s* or *-es*. If the word is only one syllable and the addition of the plural will still keep it one syllable, *-s* is usually added: kite/kites, girl/girls, scene/scenes, light/lights, toy/toys.

If another syllable is added when making the plural, *-es* is usually added: glass/glasses, wish/wishes, wrench/wrenches. If the word ends with *o* and that *o* follows a vowel, the plural is generally made by adding *-s:* rodeo/rodeos, patio/patios, radio/radios, ratio/ratios, taboo/taboos.

TIP

Accurate spelling is a matter of early drill work in school. The more you know of other languages, the more you will understand spelling patterns and variances.

If, however, the word ends with *o* and that *o* follows a consonant, the plural is generally made by adding *-es:* tomato/tomatoes, zero/zeroes, echo/echoes, potato/potatoes. (There are exceptions to this general rule—especially when musical terms are used, as in alto/altos or piano/pianos—so use your speller when in doubt.)

3. When to use *ie* or *ei*. The old school verse generally can be followed: Use *i* before *e* except after *c*, or when the word has a sound like *ay*, such as in *weigh*. This verse applies when the combination is sounded as a single vowel, but not when it is two distinct vowels: diet, science, deist, reintroduce.

4. When to double a final consonant. If the word is a single-syllable word and ends with a single final consonant, double it when adding a suffix that is also a single syllable and begins with a vowel (*-ed, -er, -ing*): trip/tripping, big/bigger, stop/stopped.

If the word ends in a single final consonant and has two or more syllables with the accent on the last syllable, double the final consonant when adding the one-syllable consonant that begins with a vowel: begin/beginning, refer/referred, occur/occurrence, omit/omitted.

If a word has two vowels in front of the final single consonant, do not double the consonant when adding the suffix: read/reader, keep/keeper (thus bookkeeping), feel/feeling, boil/boiling. If a word normally ends in two consonants, do not double the last one when adding the suffix: damp/damper, pick/picking, gulp/gulping, help/helping.

If a word ends in a single final consonant and the last syllable of the word is not stressed (the accent is earlier in the word), do not double the final consonant when adding the suf-

fix: profit/profited, jewel/jeweler, benefit/benefiting.

If the word ends in a single consonant with the accent on the last syllable, and that accent shifts forward when the suffix is added, do not double the final consonant for that suffix (but double it if the accent remains when the suffix is added): refer/reference, but referred; confer/conference, but conferring; prefer/preference, but preferred.

If a word ends in *x,* do not double the *x* when adding a suffix: box/boxing, mix/mixed, fix/fixer.

When in doubt, use your dictionary to look up the word and the form it takes when a suffix is added. A speller is less likely to contain these forms of the word.

5. Whether to keep the final *e* when adding a suffix. Generally, keep the *e* in words that end with a silent *e* when adding a suffix that begins with a consonant, but drop the *e* when adding a suffix that begins with a vowel: force/forceful/forcing, love/lovely/lovable, use/useless/usage, advise/advised/advisory. In American English, this rule is usually followed when *-ment* is added; judge/judgment, acknowledge/acknowledgment.

If the word ends in *ce* or *ge*, keep the *e* when the suffix begins with an *a* or *o* (this is to keep the sound "soft"): notice/noticeable, but noticing; manage/manageable, but managing; service/serviceable, but servicing; and courage/courageous.

In verbs, a final *ie* is changed to *y* before adding *-ing*: die/dying, lie/lying, tie/tying. A final *oe* is unchanged when adding *-ing*: canoe/canoeing, hoe/hoeing, shoe/shoeing.

For each of these general rules, it is always possible to encounter an exception. Keep your speller handy. Your confidence about sensing

---

TIP

When in doubt, look up the word in your dictionary.

---

the right spelling of a word will develop as you continue to use your speller and dictionary.

If you use a word processor with a spell-check function, use the spell-check at the conclusion of each job and after you finish revising a job. This dictionary will catch obvious typos and will force you to double-check complex words. It will not alert you to words that are spelled correctly but used wrongly: *fiend* for *friend, follow* for *following, contexts* for *contents*. To catch misspellings of this nature, you have to proofread the job both for spelling and for sense.

Poor spelling reflects badly on your boss. People who receive the letter will think less highly of her. It also reflects badly on you. Your boss might manifest her anger for your making her look foolish or ignorant, or she might try to be nice about it, hiding her anger. An occasional blooper can be forgiven, but a continued pattern of poor spelling may soon result in your transfer or worse. Your boss would much rather wait a few minutes for you to check any doubtful spelling so you can present her with work you can both take professional pride in.

CHAPTER 21
WORD DIVISION

Normally, word division is not a factor in most of your business correspondence. You type letters, memos, and reports flush left, ragged right. Whole words end a line and whole words begin the next line. By not dividing words at the end of a line, you save yourself a great deal of time. You also save yourself the possibility of making errors by dividing the word at the wrong place.

Word division becomes a factor when you have a big gap at the end of a line because the last word of that line is long and would go too far over the margin to look presentable. Rather than leave the gap, you decide to divide the word. In routine business correspondence, this may happen only ten or twenty times a week.

Word division becomes a major factor if you use a word processor for long reports and your boss wants the report justified (flush left *and* flush right). In order to fill in space for justified printing, you need to divide many words—three or four in a single paragraph.

There is a basic rule to keep in mind for word division. In America, words are divided according to pronunciation. This sometimes results in strange-looking divisions, unless you understand this rule. For instance, "knowledge" is divided into two syllables:

"knowl" and "edge." You may think the word should be divided as "know-ledge," until you think how you pronounce the word.

The rule will sometimes change the place a word is divided as the accent shifts from one syllable to another when you add prefixes or suffixes. Take, for instance, the word "re-fer." The word is divided "re-fer," with the accent on "fer." However, when you add the suffix *-ence*, the accent shifts to the first syllable and the sounds making up that first syllable change: "ref-er-ence." And if you add the suffix *-ing*, the accent stays on "fer": "re-fer-ring."

There are a number of speller-divider books published by companies that also publish dictionaries. Most of these contain about 50,000 general words. There are specialized speller-divider books for legal and medical words. If, for instance, you work in a law office, a legal speller-divider is essential.

In Chapter 20 (Spelling), I indicated how these books should be used to ensure your spelling is as accurate as possible. When dividing words, use the book to double-check any division you have any doubt about.

In the book publishing business, one of the most common reasons for sending a set of proofs back to the printer for reworking is improper word division. Today's electronic text management systems, whether a photocomposition system or your word-processing system, have hyphenation programs. If these programs are used on an automatic setting to divide words according to a program's logic, many errors will occur. The computer does not pronounce words and, therefore, does not know when a syllable shifts in human pronunciation. The computer follows a straightforward set of logical rules that is right about 85 percent of the time. It is that 15 percent of word divisions that you have to ensure are correct.

The accent on some words shifts when the word is used as a verb instead of a noun. And with the shift of accent, a shift in word division occurs: "Des-ert"—with the accent on the first syllable—is a noun, meaning "a barren region," but "de-sert"—with the accent on the last syllable—is a verb, meaning "to abandon." "Pres-ent"—with the accent on the first syllable—is a noun, meaning "a gift"; "pre-sent"—with the accent on the last syllable—is a verb, meaning "to offer or give." English is replete with examples of similar noun/verb words in which the spelling is the same, but the pronunciation is different.

The pattern of changing accents happens among variations of a word. For instance, "pre-sen-ta-tion" has a different accent from "pre-sent-able." The shift of accent changes the location of the division of the word.

As in spelling, there are several rules that will guide you correctly most of the time. And as in spelling, when in doubt, look it up. Several basic word-division rules follow:

1. A single-syllable word is not divided: "boy," "car," "time." This is true even if a suffix is added to the word, but the pronunciation continues to be a single syllable: "maimed," "rhymed," "helped," "gasped," "spelled," "mired."

2. Suffixes that are generally pronounced as a single syllable are not divided further: *-ceous, -cial, -cion, -cious, -geous, -gion, -gious, -sial, -sion, -tion,* and *-tial.* Thus, "region" is divided into "re-gion," not "re-gi-on"; "courageous" is "cou-rageous," not "cou-rage-ous."

3. A final syllable in which the only sound is an *l* or *bull* should not be divided from the preceding syllable: "pre-sent-able," not "pre-sent-a-ble"; "pos-sible," not "pos-si-ble"; "title," not "ti-tle"; "read-able," not "read-a-ble"; "people," not "peo-ple."

4. Where possible, when a vowel alone forms a syllable, make the division after the vowel: "criti-cal," not "crit-ical"; "habi-tat," not "hab-itat."

5. If pronunciation permits, word division can normally take place between two consonants when they are located between two vowels: "foun-da-tion," not "found-a-tion"; "moun-tain," not "mount-ain"; "par-ti-san," not "part-i-san."

6. Division between syllables should not be made where one syllable has only one letter. In the samples that follow, the entire word should be on one line: "able," "again," "among," "abort," "enough," "even," "item," "unite," "unit."

TIP

There is a basic rule to keep in mind for word division. In America, words are divided according to pronunciation.

TIP

Whenever possible, personal names should not be divided. When it is necessary, the name should be broken after the middle initial.

---

7. Dividing a word in which one syllable has two letters is acceptable at the end of a line, but should be avoided, if possible, at the beginning of a line: "un-sung," "il-lu-sion," "em-bassy," "am-ne-sia," but not "loss-es," "mon-ey," "flat-ly," "liv-en."

8. Where possible, when compound words are divided, they should be divided at the hyphen: "decision-making," not "deci-sion-making."

9. Words that were once compound words but have now become so standard that they are considered to be single words should be divided, as much as possible, at their natural breaks: "rough-housing," rather than "roughhous-ing"; "weather-man," rather than "weath-erman"; "harbor-master," rather than "harbormas-ter."

10. If a word has a prefix, division after the prefix is better than elsewhere in the word: "pseudo-podia," rather than "pseudopo-dia" or "pseu-dopodia"; "dis-illusion," rather than "disil-lusion"; "non-sectarian," rather than "nonsec-tarian"; "un-savory," rather than "unsa-vory."

Telephone numbers should never be divided. If the area code is in parentheses, it is possible—not preferable—to end a line with the area code and begin the next line with the telephone number.

Whenever possible, personal names should not be divided. When it is necessary, the name should be broken after the middle initial. If the name consists of the first and second initials followed by the last name, the break should be only after the second initial. Thus,

best: Jonathan R. Buckingham

first choice, if a break is needed: Jonathan R. (break) Buckingham

second choice, if a break is needed: Jonathan R. Buck-ingham

third choice: Jonathan (break) R. Bucking-ham

fourth choice: Jona-than R. Buckingham

best: T. S. Eliot

Permissible, if a break is needed: T. S. (break) Eliot

Not permissible: T. (break) S. Eliot

If abbreviations are used with figures, the figures and the abbreviations should never be separated on two different lines: 8:15 a.m.; 450 cm; 210 mi.; 25 gal.

Divide words as seldom as possible, but when you have a job in which you have to divide them throughout the job, glance through these suggestions before you begin to refresh your memory on the basic principles. Then use your speller-divider throughout the job whenever you have a question.

CHAPTER 22
COMPOUND WORDS

Compound words are a secretary's nightmare. When are they used as two words separately; when are they joined by a hyphen; when do they become so well established that they are joined into a new single word?

The most complete and easiest-to-under-stand summary of good usage for compound words that I have found is in a table in *The Chicago Manual of Style*. Rather than try to summarize the information in the table, it is clearer just to reprint the table here for your ready reference.

A SPELLING GUIDE FOR COMPOUND WORDS

TYPE COMPOUND	SIMILAR COMPOUNDS	REMARKS
Noun Forms		
master builder	master artist, master wheel *but:* mastermind, masterpiece, mastersinger, masterstroke	Spell temporary compounds with *master* open.
fellow employee	brother officer, mother church, father figure, foster child, parent organization	*Type:* word of relationship + noun. Spell all such compounds open.
decision making	problem solving, coal mining, bird watching	*Type:* object + gerund. Spell temporary compounds open. Many closed permanent compounds (e.g., *bookkeeping, dressmaking*) will be found in the dictionary. See also under Adjective Forms, below.

Type Compound	Similar Compounds	Remarks
	Noun Forms—*Continued*	
quasi corporation	quasi contract, quasi scholar, quasi union	Spell *quasi* noun compounds open. But see under Adjective Forms, below.
attorney general	postmaster general, surgeon general, judge advocate general	Safe to spell all similar compounds open.
vice-president	vice-chancellor, vice-consul *but:* viceroy, vicegerent, vice admiral	Temporary compounds with *vice-* are best hyphenated: *vice-manager, vice-chief.*
scholar-poet	author-critic, city-state, soldier-statesman	*Type:* noun + noun, representing different and equally important functions. Hyphenate.
grandfather	grandniece, grandnephew	Close up all *grand-* relatives.
brother-in-law	mother-in-law, sisters-in-law	Hyphenate all *in-laws*.
great-grandson	great-great-grandmother	Hyphenate all *great-* relatives.
self-restraint	self-knowledge, self-consciousness	Hyphenate all *self-* compounds. See also under Adjective Forms, below.
Johnny-on-the-spot	light-o'-love, Alice-sit-by-the-fire, stay-at-home, stick-in-the-mud *but:* flash in the pan, ball of fire	*Type:* combination of words including a prepositional phrase describing a character. Hyphenate any new creations.
one-half	two-thirds, four and five-sevenths *but:* thirty-one hundredths, three sixty-fourths	*Type:* spelled-out fractional number. Connect numerator and denominator with a hyphen unless either already contains a hyphen.
president-elect	senator-elect, mayor-elect *but:* county assessor elect	Hyphenate *-elect* compounds unless the name of the office is in two or more words.
headache	toothache, stomachache	Spell compounds with *-ache* solid.
checkbook	notebook, textbook, pocketbook, storybook *but:* reference book	Permanent compounds with *-book* are solid except for a few unwieldy ones.

TYPE COMPOUND	SIMILAR COMPOUNDS	REMARKS

Noun Forms—*Continued*

TYPE COMPOUND	SIMILAR COMPOUNDS	REMARKS
		Temporary compounds should be spelled open: *pattern book, recipe book.*
boardinghouse	boathouse, clubhouse, greenhouse, clearinghouse *but:* rest house, business house	Permanent compounds with *-house* are solid; temporary ones, mainly open.
ex-president	ex-husband, ex-mayor ex–corporate executive	Compounds with *ex-* meaning *former* are hyphenated (en dash when the second part is an open compound). Seldom used in formal writing, where *former* is preferred.

Adjective Forms

TYPE COMPOUND	SIMILAR COMPOUNDS	REMARKS
highly developed species	poorly seen, barely living, wholly invented, highly complex	*Type:* adverb ending in *-ly* + participle or adjective. Always open.
long-lived	much-loved, ever-fruitful, still-active	*Type:* adverb other than the *-ly* type + participle or adjective. Now usually hyphenated before the noun.
Central European countries	Old English, Scotch Presbyterian, New Testament, Civil War, Latin American	*Type:* compound formed from unhyphenated proper names. Always open. (Do not confuse with such forms as *Scotch-Irish, Austro-Hungarian.*)
sodium chloride solution	sulfuric acid, calcium carbonate	*Type:* chemical terms. Leave open.
grand prix racing	a priori, post mortem, Sturm und Drang *but:* laissez-faire	*Type:* foreign phrase used as an adjective. Leave open unless hyphenated in original language.
bluish green paint	gray blue, emerald green, coal black, reddish orange	*Type:* color term in which first element modifies the second. Leave open.
blue-green algae	red-green color blindness, black-and-white print	*Type:* color term in which elements are of equal importance. Hyphenate.

Type Compound	Similar Compounds	Remarks
	Adjective Forms—*Continued*	
self-reliant boy	self-sustaining, self-righteous, self-confident, self-effacing *but:* selfless, selfsame, unselfconscious	Hyphenate *self-* compounds whether they precede or follow the noun. See also under Noun Forms, above.
decision-making procedures	curiosity-evoking, dust-catching, thirst-quenching, dissension-producing, interest-bearing	*Type:* object + present participle. Hyphenate all before the noun and a few permanent compounds (e.g., *thought-provoking*) after the noun.
twenty-odd performances	sixty-odd, fifteen-hundred-odd, 360-odd	*Type:* cardinal number + *odd.* Hyphenate before or after the noun.
ten-foot pole	three-mile limit, 100-yard dash, one-inch margin, 10-meter band, four-year-old boy *but:* 10 percent increase	*Type:* cardinal number + unit of measurement. Hyphenate compound if it precedes noun.
well-known man	ill-favored girl, well-intentioned person *but:* very well known man; he is well known	Compounds with *well-, ill-, better-, best-, little-, lesser-,* etc., are hyphenated before the noun unless expression carries a modifier.
high-, low-level job	high-class, high-energy, low-test, low-lying *but:* highborn, highbrow, lowbred	With few exceptions, *high-* and *low-* adjectival compounds are hyphenated in any position.
matter-of-fact approach	devil-may-care attitude, a how-to book, everything is up-to-date	*Type:* phrase used as adjective. Hyphenate in any position.
quasi-public corporation	quasi-judicial, quasi-legislative, quasi-stellar	Hyphenate adjectival *quasi-* compounds whether they precede or follow the noun. But see under Noun Forms, above.
half-baked plan	half-asleep, half-blooded, half-cocked, half-timbered *but:* halfhearted, halfway	Hyphenate adjectival *half-* compounds whether they precede or follow the noun.

Type Compound	Similar Compounds	Remarks
Adjective Forms—*Continued*		
two-thirds majority	The project is three-fourths completed. He was one-fourth white.	Common fractions used as adjectives or adverbs are hyphenated.
cross-town expressway	cross-country, cross-fertile, cross-grained *but:* crossbred, crosscut, crosshatched, crosswise	Any temporary adjectival *cross-* compounds can be safely hyphenated.
all-inclusive study	all-around, all-powerful, all-out	Hyphenate *all-* compounds whether they precede or follow the noun.
coarse-grained wood	able-bodied, pink-faced, straight-sided, even-handed	*Type:* adjective + past participle derived from a noun. Hyphenate such compounds when they precede the noun. After the noun they can generally be left open.
catlike movements	fencelike, gridlike, saillike (*or* sail-like), basilicalike (*or* basilica-like) *always:* Tokyo-like, gull-like, vacuum-bottle-like	The suffix *-like* is freely used to form new compounds, which are generally spelled solid except for those formed from proper names, words ending in *ll*, and word combinations. Some also prefer to hyphenate when the base word ends in a single *l* or consists of three or more syllables.
a **tenfold** increase	twofold, multifold *but:* 25-fold	Adjectival compounds with *-fold* are spelled solid unless they are formed with figures.
a **statewide** referendum	worldwide, boroughwide, parishwide, archdiocese wide (*or* archdiocese-wide)	*Type:* word denoting a geographical, political, or social division + *-wide*. Close up unless the compound is long and cumbersome.

Words Formed with Prefixes

A few words that might be considered word-forming prefixes appear in the columns above, and most of the adjectival forms are there hyphenated. The word-forming prefixes listed below (the list is not exhaustive) generate compounds that are nearly always closed, whether they are nouns, verbs, adjectives, or adverbs. The chief exceptions to the closed-style rule are the following:

Compounds in which the second element is a capitalized word or a numeral, as *anti-Semitic, un-American, pre-1914, post-Kantian, Anti-Federalist.*

Compounds that must be distinguished from homonyms, as *re-cover, un-ionized,* sometimes *re-create.*

Compounds in which the second element consists of more than one word, as *pre-latency-period* therapy, *non-English-speaking* people, *pre–Civil War.* (In the last, note the en dash, used with an open compound.)

A few compounds in which the last letter of the prefix is the same as the first letter of the word following. Examples of these appear below.

Newly invented compounds of the last type tend to be treated in hyphenated style when they first appear and then to be closed up when they have become more familiar. This may happen, for example, to coinages like *infra-area* and *meta-analysis,* as it already has to *intraarterial.* (For *meta-analysis,* however, a better choice would be *metanalysis,* since the combining prefix also exists in the form *met-.*) In addition to familiarity, appearance also influences the retention of hyphens, and it is never wrong to keep a hyphen so as to avoid misleading or puzzling forms (e.g., *non-native, anti-intellectual*).

Note also that when a prefix stands alone, it carries a hyphen: *over- and underused, macro- and microeconomics.*

PREFIX	EXAMPLES
ante-	anteroom, antediluvian, antenatal
anti-	anticlerical, antihypertensive, *but* anti-inflammatory, anti-utopian, anti-hero
bi-	bivalent, biconvex, binomial
bio-	bioecology, biophysical
co-	coauthor, coordinate, coeditor, *but* co-edition, co-opt, co-op, co-worker
counter-	counterclockwise, countermeasures, countercurrent, counterblow
extra-	extraterrestrial, extrafine
infra-	infrasonic, infrastructure
inter-	interrelated, intertidal, interregnum
intra-	intraarterial, intrazonal, intracranial
macro-	macroeconomics, macrosphere, macromolecular
meta-	metalanguage, metagalaxy, metaethical, metastable
micro-	microminiaturized, microimage, micromethod
mid-	midocean, midtown, midgut
mini-	minibus, miniskirt, minibike
non-	nonviolent, nonperson, nonplus, nonnative (*or* non-native)
over-	overlong, overeager, overanalyzed

Prefix	Examples
post- ("after")	postdoctoral, postface, postwar, postparturition
pre-	preempt, precognition, preconference, premalignant
pro-	progovernment, procathedral, procephalic
pseudo-	pseudopregnancy, pseudoclassic, pseudoheroic
re-	reedit, reunify, redigitalize, reexamine
semi-	semiopaque, semiconductor, *but* semi-independent, semi-indirect
sub-	subjacent, subbasement, subcrustal
super-	supertanker, superhigh (frequency), superpose
supra-	supranational, suprarenal, supraliminal
trans-	transoceanic, transmembrane, transsocietal
ultra-	ultrafiche, ultramontane, ultraorganized
un-	unfunded, unchurched, uncoiffed, unneutered
under-	underused, undersea, underpowered, underreport

CHAPTER 23

ABBREVIATIONS

Every professional and business specialty develops its own set of abbreviations. Whether law or medicine, chemistry or architecture, shoes or space vehicles, each specialty has its own technical vocabulary. Often-used terms within that special vocabulary get shortened or abbreviated.

If you are new to the vocabulary, the abbreviations can seem threatening. You do not know what they mean, you do not know how to use them or when to use them, you do not know whether you are using the right one in the right place. But, as with any specialized vocabulary, you will soon feel quite at home with the abbreviations as well as with the words they represent. There are only a limited number of them, and they usually appear over and over again.

Make up a list of abbreviations used with regularity in your boss's correspondence. After the first dozen or two entries, the addition of new entries will occur only seldomly. Look them up in a dictionary (if they do not appear in the list that follows). If you cannot find one in the dictionary, ask him what it means and when it is used.

Several general statements follow about abbreviations in general.

LATIN ABBREVIATIONS

Many abbreviations came originally from Latin. If the Latin abbreviation is still used, it is more often than not in Roman (regular) typeface, rather than in italics or underlined. This is true, for instance, of etc. and et al., as well as vide, N.B., i.e., and e.g.

The abbreviations and their meanings are: Etc. from *et cetera*, meaning "and the rest" or "and so forth"; et al. from *et alii*, meaning "and others" (people, not things); vide,

meaning "see" (a reference to a similar statement elsewhere); N.B. from *nota bene*, meaning "note well" or "pay particular attention"; i.e. from *id est*, meaning "that is"; and e.g. from *exempli gratia*, meaning "for example" or "for instance."

However, modern English usage is moving away from the use of these Latin abbreviations. The English words are used in their place: and so on, and so forth; and others; see;

note; that is, or I mean; for example, for instance, or here are some examples. The average business reader will readily understand the English expression, whereas he may miss the precise nuance of the Latin abbreviation. Using the English form makes for better clarity in business correspondence and avoids literary pretentiousness.

Probably the only universally known Latin abbreviation is etc. Overuse of etc. indicates a lack of thinking through of all the facets of a subject and hiding that lack of preciseness behind the catchall abbreviation.

COMPANY NAMES AND ORGANIZATIONS

You will probably use abbreviations in company names, of companies, and of organizations more than any other kind of abbreviation. It is important to develop a consistent style for these abbreviations. Then you do not have to think about how to make the abbreviation each time you encounter the need to use one.

Company names often include one or more of the following as part of the formal company name: Bro., Bros., Co., Corp., Inc., Ltd., &, and in Spanish or French companies, S.A., Inc., and Ltd. usually follow a comma. However, many corporations no longer use the comma to separate Inc. from the rest of the name. Look at the company's letterhead or its listing in a business or trade directory to see what is done by that particular company.

The full title, including Inc., Ltd., or Corp., is used on the envelope and in the address section of the letter. In the body of the letter, however, Inc. or Ltd. is usually dropped when the company is referred to. This book is printed by Doubleday, but in writing to the editor for this book, the company was addressed on the envelope as Doubleday & Company, Inc.

The ampersand (&) is used only when the company itself uses it in its title.

Many companies abbreviate their names to initials. These abbreviations are often better known than the full name of the company: Radio Corporation of America/RCA; International Business Machines Corporation/IBM;

National Cash Register Corporation/NCR; Trans World Airlines/TWA. These abbreviations can be used without further defining them. They are normally used without periods: TWA, not T.W.A.

The same is true of government agencies, associations, unions, and other groups. Some are so well known that the abbreviation alone is enough; however, some should be used only after the full name of the organization has first been written out in full. Thus, TVA, YMCA, NBC, AT&T, OPEC, and NATO can probably be used without first writing out the name of the organization (Tennessee Valley Authority, Young Men's Christian Association, National Broadcasting Company, American Telephone & Telegraph Company, Organization of Petroleum Exporting Countries, and North Atlantic Treaty Organization). However, if your letter refers to ASEA, NCRWS, or ABC, you should write out the full name of the organization, follow it with the abbreviation in parentheses, and then use the abbreviation throughout the rest of the letter: American Solar Energy Association (ASEA); National Campaign for Radioactive Waste Safety (NCRWS); and American Beagle Club (ABC). With ABC, it is especially important to define the abbreviation by using the full name of the organization since most readers would automatically assume ABC means American Broadcasting Company.

Government agencies are initial-prone. If your work includes constant reference to or interaction with a number of government agencies, you should keep a list of the agencies and their initial abbreviations. The Government Printing Office (GPO) publishes an annual directory of all agencies, with their abbreviations, addresses, and chief personnel with their titles.

TITLES AND FORMS OF ADDRESS

You will continually use abbreviations for titles and forms of address of people to whom you write or write about. If a title is used before a name, it is spelled out fully when the person's last name is used alone: General Eisenhower, Lieutenant Commander Jones, Congressman Udall, Senator Percy. If the person's first name, first name and middle initial, or initials are used, the title is normally abbreviated: Gen. Dwight D. Eisenhower, Lt. Cdr. John Q. Jones, Rep. Morris Udall, Sen. Charles Percy. Only if you were in a naval office would you abbreviate Lieutenant Commander to LCDR; most people in a civilian setting would not understand that particular in-group abbreviation.

Some forms of address are always abbreviated, whether the full name or only the last name is used: Mr., Mrs., Miss, Ms., M., MM., Mme., Mlle., Dr., Sr., Sra., Srta.

If the title includes a reference to Reverend or Honorable, the word is spelled out in full if it follows "the": the Honorable Frank M. Wright; the Reverend Robert C. Parkinson; the Reverend Dr. Hightower; the Very (Most) (Right) Reverend Thomas P. Smith. But in many other cases, the title is abbreviated when used with the full name: Hon. Frank M. Wright; Rev. Robert C. Parkinson; Rt. Rev. Thomas P. Smith; Rev. Dr. Richard S. Hightower. The abbreviation is not used with just the last name: Dear Mr. Wright, not Dear Hon. Wright; Dear Bishop Smith, not Dear Rt. Rev. Smith; Dear Dr. Hightower, not Dear Rev. Dr. Hightower; Dear Mr. Parkinson, not Dear Rev. Parkinson. If Mr. Parkinson is a Roman Catholic or Episcopalian priest, it is permissible to write Dear Father Parkinson or Dear Fr. Parkinson.

Titles or degrees, when used after a name, follow a comma: John M. Packard, Sr.; John M. Packard, Jr.; Mrs. John M. Packard, Sr.; Richard B. Thorne, M.D.; the Rev. Thomas P. Ambleer, D.D.; William R. Orcutt, Esq. The only exception to this is when III or IV is a part of the name: John M. Packard III. These abbreviations are never used with just the last name: Mr. Packard, Jr., is not correct.

Esq. (for Esquire) is used in America to denote a lawyer. It is used only with the first name, middle initial, and last name; never with Mr. or Ms. Thus, Ellen S. Porter, Esq., is correct; Ms. Ellen S. Porter, Esq., is not. She would be addressed as Dear Ms. Porter.

The Dr. in front of a name is dropped if

the degree follows the name: Richard B. Thorne, M.D., not Dr. Richard B. Thorne, M.D.

If you use a company or organizational title on the envelope or as part of the address section of the letter, the person's title follows the full name and is separated by a comma; the social form of address (Mr., Ms., Dr.) is not used when a title follows the name: Robert S. Rodney, President, not Mr. Robert S. Rod-ney, President; Mary K. Winters, Comptroller, not Ms. Mary K. Winters, Comptroller.

In most businesses, Dr. is not used as the normal way of addressing executives, even though they may have earned degrees or honorary degrees. Dr. is always used with medical and dental personnel; it is usually used by religious personnel, even though it may be an honorary doctorate. It is usually used in academic circles only if it is an earned doctorate.

METRIC ABBREVIATIONS

Metric measurements are used in scientific writing. Increasingly, they are used in applications where English measurements were once used; you now buy wine by the liter instead of the quart or gallon. Metric abbreviations are not followed by a period: meter/m; gram/gm; centimeter/cm; cubic centimeter/cc.

ENGLISH ABBREVIATIONS

Traditional English abbreviations, however, are followed by a period: inch/in.; foot/ft.; mile/mi.; gallon/gal.; cubic yard/cu. yd.; ounce/oz.

GEOGRAPHY AND LOCATIONS

The custom now is to use the Postal Service abbreviations for states rather than the older conventions: CA, not Calif. or Cal.; CO, not Colo.; MA, not Mass. When standing alone in the body of a letter or report (not combined with the name of a city), the state should be spelled out in full.

City names are generally not abbreviated in letters: Fort Wayne, not Ft. Wayne. The most noticeable exception to this is a city that includes the word Saint: St. Paul, St. Louis. However, spelling out the word Saint is entirely acceptable.

Normally, the names of countries are spelled out in full, although Russia is often abbreviated to USSR.

In letters, the names of streets in addresses are usually spelled out: Avenue, Drive, Lane, Street, Boulevard, Place, Road. If the address includes a quadrant of the city (NE, SW, NW, SE), that designation usually follows the street and is abbreviated: 1505 K Street, SE; but 837 Central Park West. N., E., S., or W. goes before a street address and usually takes a period: 83 N. Elm Street.

TIME

Months are usually spelled out in full, as are the days of the week. In typing, the time of the day is usually lowercase (small letters) and not underlined: 8:15 a.m.; 5:45 p.m. These are abbreviations borrowed from Latin: a.m. (*ante meridiem*) means ''before noon''; p.m. (*post meridiem*) means ''after noon.''

Usually, if periods are used in abbreviation, there are no spaces after those periods within the abbreviation itself: a.m., not a. m.;

Ph.D., not Ph. D.; U.S., not U. S.; i.e., not i. e. However, use a space between the initials of a person's name: T. S. Eliot, not T.S. Eliot.

Abbreviations are normally used in tables that are not normally used in the body of a letter or report. Thus, in the report you would spell out the months, but in a table in the report you might use the following abbreviations to save space, especially at the heads of columns: Ja F Mr Ap My Je Jl Ag S O N D or the more familiar Jan Feb Mar Apr May June July Aug Sept Oct Nov Dec. Much depends on the amount of space you have available.

CHAPTER 24
POSTAL
SERVICE FORMS

Although you may use alternative methods of sending correspondence and small packages—ranging from air-express services to internal electronic mail—you will use the United States Postal Service (USPS) as the standard means of sending mail. The basic reasons are cost and convenience. The cost of sending a nonpriority letter is much less when it is sent through the Postal Service than when it is sent by air express. At the time of writing, it was 5,500% less! A letter can be dropped in a handy mail chute near the elevator on your floor or in a convenient mailbox at a nearby corner. You do not need to make special arrangements to have a first-class letter picked up, nor do you need to make a special trip to the post office to mail it.

You should ask the post office for a booklet entitled *Mailers Guide* that describes the mail services the USPS offers. If, for instance, your company is a nonprofit organization, there are special rates for sending bulk mail. With those rates there are conditions, which include packaging the mail in zip-code sequence. If your business sends out thousands of bills to customers, there are lower first-class rates, provided the mail is packaged in a certain way. Your business can get a bulk-rate

permit, which allows for the printing of bulk-rate indicia on an envelope or self-mailer (a folder, brochure, or catalog that has an address label placed on the piece itself; a self-mailer is not put into an envelope). This saves having to affix a postage stamp to each piece.

If your company is a large one, the mailing department and others in the company will have the responsibility for securing special permits, keeping up with changing postal regulations and rates, and preparing bulk mail according to USPS requirements. However, it is important for you to know about available USPS services. You can never predict when that knowledge will be very useful.

There are several USPS services that you will use from time to time. To do so, you need to fill out USPS forms, which can be obtained from a postal clerk at the post office; get a sizable supply so you can fill them out at your desk rather than at the post office. You—or someone from the mail room—will have to take the letter or package with the completed forms to the post office when you want to mail it. You can type in the information asked for on the forms. If you make a mistake in the recipient's name and address on a multicopy form, such as Express-Mail forms, retype a new form rather than erasing since the third copy is the mailing label. If you fill the form out by hand, use a ballpoint pen and press hard.

EXPRESS MAIL

USPS Express-Mail services were discussed in Chapter 6, but some discussion of the forms involved is needed. One of the forms is a Post-Office-to-Post-Office Express-Mail form, to be used if the addressee has a post-office box. The box number should be included in the "AT:" section. The letter itself, or a notice indicating that the post office is holding the piece, will be placed in the recipient's box soon after the piece arrives in the post office. You may wish to call the addressee to alert him to watch for the piece since it will not be delivered to his office.

If the addressee does not have a post-office box, you should call him to make sure he goes to the post office to pick up the piece. Usually, he can call ahead to the clerk at the Express-Mail window to find out if the piece has arrived.

There is also a Post-Office-to-Addressee Express-Mail form. The USPS will deliver a piece sent with this form to the addressee.

Keep your customer receipt copies of Express-Mail forms. Put them in the file together with the copy of the letter or forwarding memo you sent with the piece. If the piece does not arrive when scheduled, you will need to give the form number to the USPS in order to trace the whereabouts of the package. The USPS treats Express Mail in the same way it does certified mail, with some of the same paperwork, so the tracing procedures are well defined.

For a small extra charge, you can request a return receipt that shows you that the addressee has in fact received the piece.

The USPS has an Express-Mail stamp, which carries the face value of the current basic rate for a Post-Office-to-Addressee piece. If your piece is heavier than that allowed under the basic weight rate, you will have to have the piece weighed and rated individually at the post office or by your mail room.

RETURN RECEIPT

For registered, certified, insured, collect-on-delivery (COD), and Express-Mail pieces, it is possible to have the USPS provide you with a return receipt. This is a postcard form that is affixed to the envelope or package. The addressee must sign the card when it is delivered, and the USPS mails that card back to you as evidence that the package was delivered and actually received by the addressee or his agent.

You fill in the information on the front of the return-receipt form, typing or printing your own name and address and the additional items on the back. The postal clerk will fill in the costs for the service you choose: (a) show to whom and date delivered, (b) show to whom, date, and address of delivery, or (c) restricted delivery to only the person who is named as the addressee. You also fill in the type of service requested: (a) registered, (b) certified, (c) insured, (d) COD, or (e) Express Mail. And you fill in the form number from the registered, certified, insured, COD, or Express-Mail form. This serves as a cross-check to ensure that the proper piece was delivered and provides tracing information if it is needed.

The USPS has the person to whom the piece is delivered sign the form. The delivering post office writes in the date of delivery and places its stamp on the card, together with the initials of the postal employee who made the delivery. If the addressee refuses to accept delivery, that action is noted and both the card and the piece are returned to you.

When you use the return-receipt form, be sure to print or type "Return Receipt Requested" close to the type of service number on the front of the piece. The type of service is either registered, certified, insured, COD, or Express Mail, and the type of service number is the number of the form you use to designate that service.

REGISTERED MAIL

Registered mail is the most secure method of sending mail through the USPS. It is carried in locked mail pouches and held in a post-office safe until delivery. The post office that accepts a registered piece issues a registry number, which it enters on the form.

You fill in the bottom half of the registered-mail form, giving the addressee's name and address and your own, plus the value of the article, if any, and whether you want postal insurance for it. The postal clerk fills in the top half of the form, indicating the charges for the services you request: registered fee, postage, special-delivery fee, return-receipt fee, restricted-delivery fee, special-handling fee, or airmail. Airmail is important if the piece is being sent overseas.

Since a registered piece is so important, you will usually request a return receipt along with registered service. Registered service is often used by companies that send jewelry or watches through the mail. Your copies of the registered-mail form and the return receipt should be kept with the correspondence so you can prove shipment and delivery should any question arise in the future.

CERTIFIED MAIL

Certified mail provides a receipt to the sender for a first-class letter and a record of delivery at the delivering post office. Unlike registered mail, no insurance of the article is possible. The bottom block with the form number and the words "Certified Mail" is affixed to the article itself. If you are also requesting a return receipt, type or print the words "Return Receipt Requested" near this number.

You fill in the name and address of the addressee; the postal clerk fills in the charges for the services you request: postage, certified fee, special-delivery fee, and restricted-delivery fee. You keep the top portion of the form after the postal clerk has stamped it; it serves as your receipt. The number is to be used if tracing is required.

The USPS attaches a yellow form to the article. The addressee has to sign for the article, and the USPS keeps the yellow form as part of its record. If you have requested a return receipt, the addressee also has to sign the return-receipt postcard form and that is mailed by the USPS to you.

TIP

You should ask the post office for a booklet entitled *Mailers Guide* that describes the mail services the USPS offers.

INSURED MAIL

You can insure an article you send by USPS. Rates and limits can be obtained from a postal clerk. Mail can be insured when it is sent either to U.S. or international addresses. There is an insured-mail form for articles with greater value.

The postal clerk enters the charges on the top portion of the front of the form. The bottom portion—the form number and the words "U.S. MAIL INSURED"—is affixed to the article. If you are requesting a return receipt, print or type "Return Receipt Requested" on the piece near the location of these numbers. You fill in the name and address of the addressee on the back of the top portion of the form. After the postal clerk has stamped the form, you keep it with the correspondence about the article. This part of the completed form is evidence of your being insured should you need to make a claim. Keep the form at least until you know the article has arrived safely.

There is an insured-mail form for articles with lesser value. You fill in the back side of the form with the addressee's name and address. The postal clerk fills in the front side of the form with charges for postage and fees. The postal clerk stamps the package or envelope "INSURED" and gives you the receipt. You should retain the receipt until you are sure the package has arrived.

First-class mail and parcels can be insured. Registered mail, COD mail, and Express Mail can also be insured. Certified mail cannot be insured.

COLLECT-ON-DELIVERY (COD) MAIL

If you mail an article that is for sale and you want the addressee to pay the USPS for the article upon delivery, you can send the article COD. The USPS will in turn forward to you in the form of a money order the amount collected from the addressee to pay for the article. You have set the price of the article. The addressee also has to pay COD handling charges and the fee for the money order. If the USPS has to return the article to you because the addressee has changed his mind about wanting the article and refuses to pay for it, there is no extra charge to you since the possibility of such refusal has been factored into the COD fee.

The COD form is a stiff tag that has four perforated sections. The postal clerk puts in the COD number on each of the four sections. The first or outermost section is your receipt. You fill in the name and address of the addressee and how much is due you for the article. The postal clerk fills in the charges: COD fee, postage, and any special-handling, special-delivery, restricted-delivery, or return-receipt fees. You usually do not need a return receipt with a COD article since payment in the form of a USPS money order will be proof of receipt.

The second section is the Mailing Office Coupon. You fill in the name and address of the addressee and how much is due you for the article. The postal clerk fills in the rest. This coupon is retained by the sending post office for a year in case there is any claim.

The third section is the Delivery Employee Coupon. This is filled in by the delivering post office. It shows the date of delivery and whether the article was refused by the addressee. The coupon is retained by the delivering post office for two years in case there is any claim.

The fourth or innermost section is the main mailing tag. You fill in the addressee's name and address as well as your own. The charges (funds to be sent to you) and the money-order fee are entered on the front of the section. You enter the charges and the post-office clerk enters the money-order fee. The back of the section is signed by the addressee when he receives the article and pays the charges. The money order will be only for the charges. The money order and this section will be returned to you by the USPS as proof of delivery and as payment for the article.

SPECIAL DELIVERY

You can request special delivery or special handling of an article at the time you mail it. There are no special forms to fill out to secure either of these services. You can type "SPECIAL DELIVERY" on the envelope; or you can buy a rubber stamp that has these words; or you can ask the postal clerk to stamp the words on the envelope when you mail it.

Special-delivery service is provided by the post office at the place of delivery. Service may include delivery at times beyond the normal delivery hours and Sunday and holiday delivery. The size of the local post office determines the extent of the special-delivery services.

SPECIAL HANDLING

Special-handling service is available for parcel-post packages only. It includes priority handling within the postal system so far as possible, but it does not include special delivery to the addressee from the delivering post office.

CUSTOMS DECLARATIONS

Many overseas countries require a customs declaration containing the contents and value of the package. There are two customs-declaration forms used by the USPS: One is a simple form for packages of modest value; the other is a more complex form for parcel-post packages of greater value. The postal clerk will tell you which form to use, depending on the country to which you are mailing the article. The detailed rules governing customs declarations are continually changing as individual countries change their laws and regulations. The USPS issues current guides for its postal clerks that cover country-by-country requirements.

Postal customs-declaration forms have been standardized by the International Postal Union. French and English are the two world languages used on all customs-declaration forms.

You fill in the front with a brief description of the contents. You mark whether it is a gift or a sample. You indicate the value; and since you are sending the article from the United States, you indicate the value in U.S. dollars (such as, US$15.90). Because many other countries also call their currency "dollars" and use the dollar sign ($), it is customary in international business to indicate which kind of dollar is connoted. There are Canadian dollars (C$15.90), New Zealand dollars (NZ$15.90), Australian dollars (A$15.90), Hong Kong dollars (HK$15.90), Singapore dollars (S$15.90), Malay dollars (M$15.90), and many others, including Liberia, Guyana, Bermuda, Trinidad & Tobago, and Western

Samoa. It is especially important if you are sending your article to one of these "dollar" countries that you specify US$ in your value declaration to avoid confusing the customs officer in the receiving country.

There is a more complex parcel-post customs-declaration form. On this form, the value is called for in US$ amounts, since it is a USPS-produced form for an article being posted from the United States. The postal clerk fills in the information in the shaded boxes. When you have completed your sec-

tions of the form and the postal clerk has completed his and has stamped the form, tear off the first two copies and place them in the envelope (which is a part of the form kit). Peel off the cover of the back side of the form envelope, uncovering a sticky surface, and affix the envelope to the front of the package. The reason for the extra declaration forms is that different countries have different paperwork regulations for incoming parcels. This kit provides enough forms to meet the requirements of any country.

ZIP-CODE DIRECTORY

The USPS issues a zip-code directory annually. This directory contains all the zip codes in the country—by street and house or business number, in larger communities. You can purchase a copy of the USPS zip-code directory at any post office or from a Government Printing Office Bookstore.

CHAPTER 25

SECRETARIAL ORGANIZATIONS AND ASSOCIATIONS

There are a number of professional organizations and associations for secretaries. Some of these organizations are national, but have local chapters. Some are general in nature; some are related to specific specialties of secretarial work.

I urge you to join one or more of these professional organizations. Through membership you will meet other secretaries in other firms, developing your own "network" for future professional development. If at some time you sense a change of company would be to your benefit, someone you have met through a professional secretarial organization might be able to suggest a splendid, unadvertised opening at another company.

Membership will also provide you with opportunities to learn how to increase your professionalism. At meetings and seminars sponsored by such organizations, you can learn more about quality secretarial practice. Some of these organizations publish newsletters, seminar reports, books, and conduct courses that include information on enhancing secretarial skills.

Today as we strive for equal pay for equal work, secretarial salaries are being scrutinized. These organizations provide effective lobbying at national, state, and industry levels for upgrading the pay and recognition due to secretaries. Whether you are female or male, you can only benefit as the job-enhancement efforts of these organizations are successful. The effectiveness of an organization's lobbying efforts is partly dependent on the size and scope of its membership. Your membership gives such an organization a little more influence, which the organization can use to better the status of all secretaries.

Visually Impaired Secretarial Transcribers Association (Blind)
337 S. Sherman Drive, Indianapolis, IN 46201
(317) 356-7725

To protect and improve the training, employment, and related interests of visually impaired persons in secretarial work. Library and placement service. Newsletter. Convention: annual.

Architectural Secretaries Association
1735 New York Avenue, NW
Washington, DC 20006
(303) 751-7844

To advance the professionalism of secretaries employed by licensed architects. Local chapters. Quarterly journal (*Architectural Secretary*). Convention: annual.

TIP

Through membership in a professional organization you will meet other secretaries in other firms, developing your own "network" for future professional development.

National Secretaries Association
Crown Center, Suite G-10
2440 Pershing Road, Kansas City, MO 64108
(816) 474-5755

Professional organization of secretaries. Local chapters. Grants CPS certificate (Certified Professional Secretary) upon completion of professional examinations. Sponsors Secretaries Week. Provides education and professional development. 10/year magazine (*The Secretary*). Convention: annual.

National Association of Legal Secretaries
3005 E. Skelly Drive, Suite 120, Tulsa, OK 74105
(918) 749-6423

Sponsors legal secretarial training courses, leading to PLS (Professional Legal Secretary) certificate. Local chapters. Bimonthly publication (*The Docket*). Convention: annual.

Congressional Staff Club
Box 2000
Longworth House Office Building
Washington, DC 20515
(202) 225-3821

For secretarial and other employees of the U.S. Congress. Provides social and professional improvement programs. Weekly bulletin. Meeting: monthly.

Executive Women International
2188 Highland Drive, Suite 203
Salt Lake City, UT 84106
(801) 486-3121

For women employed as executive secretaries or in administrative positions. Local chapters. Quarterly publication (*Times*). Convention: annual.

National Association of Educational Office Personnel
1902 Association Drive, Reston, VA 20911
(703) 860-2888

For secretaries and others employed in offices of schools, colleges, universities, district and state departments of education. Local chapters. Provides professional training and summer institutes. Publications: quarterly journals and books. Convention: annual.

National Association of Executive Secretaries
9401 Lee Highway, Suite 210, Fairfax, VA 22031
(703) 273-2988

Dedicated to give added stature and additional benefits to the executive secretary. Local chapters. Monthly magazine (*Exec-u-tary*). Convention: annual.

National Association of Government Secretaries
5143 Summit Drive, Fairfax, VA 22030
(202) 631-9473

Seeks to improve members' qualifications for better jobs in government. Monthly newsletter. Convention: annual.

National Association of Rehabilitation Secretaries
1522 K Street NW, Washington, DC 20005

Specializes in training and job potential for handicapped persons to serve as secretaries. Local chapters. Job service. Quarterly newsletter. Convention: annual.

National Collegiate Association for Secretaries
College of Business Administration
University of South Carolina
Columbia, SC 29208
(803) 777-6419

For secretarial students in two- and four-year degree-granting institutions. Local chapters. Semiannual newsletter. Convention: biennial.

The Creative Secretary
Executive Reports Corporation
Englewood Cliffs, NJ 07632

A bimonthly letter for secretaries, filled with ideas, case studies, suggestions, and experiences of successful secretaries in many types and sizes of businesses.

INDEX